NATURAL NETWORKING

Building your professional network,
without pain.

Kevin Doolan and Alexis Caught

COPYRIGHT NOTICE

ISBN: 1495200027
ISBN 13: 9781495200021
Library of Congress Control Number: 2014900941
CreateSpace Independent Publishing Platform
North Charleston, South Carolina

"If you can imagine your perfect future, see it clearly in your mind, then you are more than half the way there."

KEVIN'S OPENING WORDS...

Dedicated to my incredible wife Debbie whose constant support and encouragement has been the foundation upon which I have built my life and my wonderful daughter Kimberley who continually makes me a proud father. I also need to thank my friends and mentors who have shaped my journey – in particular, Lorraine Kilborn, Imogen Lee, Moray McLaren, Zelinda Bennett, Ashish Nanda and Michele DeStefano.

ALEXIS WOULD LIKE TO THANK...

My strong and supportive parents, for empowering me and teaching me to aim high and work on. My first employers, Neal and Simon at DesignBridge, for spotting something in me and setting me on my career path. Finally, to my friends who have put up with me questioning them, given me reassurance along the way and most importantly, kept me grounded, sane and smiling.

INTRODUCTION

If you have ever been put off by books that promise to teach you how to use small talk then this book is for you. It's about working in your own style, using your strengths and making sure that you feel safe, relaxed and confident. Then that attitude will come across to everyone that you meet.

Whether you want to meet new clients, are looking for a job, need to raise your profile, meet new people or want a career change then building a powerful network is absolutely the best way to achieve your desires.

This book is designed to help young, and not so young, professionals benefit from creating a great network of contacts. Building this network will transform your opportunities, allow you to meet people who share your interests and who will make a real difference to your success – not just in your career but in the richness and variety of the personal relationships that you build.

Business networking is about identifying and connecting with exactly the right people in ways that work for all concerned. The best networkers *do not* fit into a particular type, they can adapt fluidly and make things work for them. So put aside any ideas you have of becoming an outgoing, social butterfly. You should never think that you have to change yourself or your personality in order to succeed, in fact that's a great recipe for failure! Brilliant networking is about using your own interests to create connections with people who share your passion. It's natural and enjoyable, and you are going to learn how to do this in ways that work with your own personality and style.

Great networkers benefit in the following ways:

- Getting to know people for job opportunities

- Raising their personal profile

- Finding out what's going on in their areas of interest

- Meeting new and interesting people

- Developing new clients

- Making lifelong friends

This book is not just about "how to network a room", although it covers that too. It is about the whole process of how professionals like lawyers, accountants, management consultants, actuaries, marketing executives, branding experts, architects, investment bankers – in fact *anyone* with a professional expertise – can lay the foundations of a really strong, successful and rewarding career. Very many professional people detest small talk and "working a room". So this book shows both how to ease any fears that may interfere with face to face networking *and* how to create a powerful network without ever having to make small talk in a roomful of strangers.

The areas covered include:

- How to harness the power of career focus, and why this is the most important step in networking

- How to meet exactly the right people for you

- What to say, so that people will really like you and want to meet you again. (There's a simple trick to this)

- Why people connect – what's going on in their minds – and how to use the power of empathy

- Networking online, in particular how to get the most out of LinkedIn and Twitter

- How to, very comfortably, network in a roomful of strangers (especially if that worries you) – and how to network without ever having to "work a room" (if you really want to avoid it)

- How to appear and actually be more confident (another tried and tested trick!)

- How you can actively manage your reputation – both online and off – using an understanding of what personal brand means

- Why most networking advice is just plain wrong!

This will be a fun and enjoyable journey, we aim to keep everything tangible and simple to follow – creating no great laborious tasks, breaking networking down into manageable chunks. You are going to see your connections grow and really understand how to benefit from that. You will enjoy a richer and more successful life and make friends, even life partners.

There will be a focus on making sure that you see small successes at every stage so that you grow in confidence and genuinely enjoy building a supportive, powerful and truly global network of "business friends". You will learn in particular why anyone (particularly those senior people whom you might think would have no interest in meeting and talking to you) will positively enjoy engaging with you ,whether that's online or face to face…

…and you will learn "The Secret of Universal Attraction" – which is a bold promise. This actually works as the thousands of young (and not quite so young) professionals that have been taught this can attest. We just wish someone had taught us this, when we were starting out in our careers!

So let's start to enjoy our networking journey and alter the course of your future life.

TABLE OF CONTENTS

A ROAD MAP FOR THIS BOOK

The benefits of being well networked are substantial and very valuable. It means being able to connect with the people who are most important to you in your job, your career aspirations and in your personal life. There is a relatively simple process for enabling great networking and this chapter will serve as a guide to all of the steps.

Great networking is about going on a journey. So, it is most important that you set off in the right direction. The very first step is to look at FOCUS –professionals will typically spend far too little time on this, and it shows in poor results. Most people spend more time planning their holidays than they do on working out what their career focus is going to be. It's not about your profession of lawyer, accountant or whatever. That's too general. In order to be really successful you need to find out what subjects really interest you, then use those as the foundation for your networking activity.

THE POWER OF FOCUS – the importance of narrowing down your area or areas of expertise and interest. Finding your passion. It is like rocket fuel for success!

Once you have worked out your focus then the next stage – TARGET – is really easy. Once you know what you want to do with your professional life we can show you where you go (in real life and online) to meet exactly the right people. It's important to have narrowed your focus because this means that you are going to spend much less time, but on the right people. In the Target stage you spend a little time working out who are the people that are going to be most useful to you in your future career and help you to achieve your personal goals.

TARGET – having a clear focus makes it really easy to identify your targets, the people with whom you need to be in contact. Someone who has chosen the healthy eating sector, retailing, the cosmetics industry or marine conservation has made the next stage really easy, because they can very easily find people who share those interests.

So far so good. Many people then become frozen by the next stage – making the FIRST CONTACT. There are in fact so many easy ways to make an approach that we will never want you to "cold call" anyone, ever! This is where you will really start to enjoy yourself. You might arrange for a good friend to introduce you to a target or you might join in a conversation with them online. There are many ways to remove any worries that you have which might put you off, at this stage it's about gently thinking of ways you might connect. In later Chapters we look at the real power of networking – *having someone that you know really well, introduce you to someone that you would like to know.*

FIRST CONTACT – how do you sit next to the target person that you want to meet or how can you be introduced online? Why would they want to meet you anyway?

Next we look at the science behind FIRST IMPRESSIONS – what do people think about you, when they first meet you? Interestingly, there are three dimensions to a first impression – and you can influence all of them. Even though these three factors have long been recognised, recent advances in neuroscience and an ability to scan the brain to see what areas are most active, have brought real evidence of what is going through someone's mind when they meet you.

FIRST IMPRESSIONS – people who meet you are going to judge how happy you are, how competent you are and your level of confidence. How can you change the impression that you make?

People have very common, shared, fears about what might go wrong when they try to network a roomful of people that they do not know. This includes finding themselves stranded on their own, being stuck talking to one person, being in a conversation that completely dries up, finding themselves meeting someone famous or really important and not knowing what to say or do. It's no wonder that so many people – particularly professional people who are used to knowing what they are doing and being in control – hate the idea of face to face networking. This chapter shows you the "tricks" of networking a room – the real physical issues about approaching and engaging with people, moving away and talking to others. There is also *an explanation of the purpose of networking* – this will surprise and delight you, because once you understand this you will find almost all of the pressure of networking is removed. Finally, you will be shown how to network naturally and enjoyably if you are an introvert or otherwise hate the idea of "working a room".

NETWORKING A ROOM – learn how the experts make it easy for themselves and also learn how to network just as effectively if you are an introvert and HATE networking with a room full of people that you do not know.

It may surprise you, but there are easily learned techniques which will transform the way in which you talk with other people and completely alter the impact that you have upon them. All of the worries you may have had about needing to impress people, have great and funny stories or expertise to display are completely misplaced. This chapter teaches you an alternative approach that is much easier and more likely to have a better impact on the people that you meet. It shows how to engage with people in ways that will make them like you, find you really interesting and want to see you again. This is such a valuable, and easily learned, skill that it is surprising how few professionals are taught this as part of their core skill set. It includes *the Secret of Universal Attraction.*

MAKING AN IMPACT – what to say when you meet people so that they will like you and want to meet you again – and learn "The Secret of Universal Attraction"!

What do the best brands do to raise their profile, add value, deliver on a promise and create loyalty? In this chapter you will learn how brands create their success and how, as an individual, you can use those principles to create a personal brand for yourself. Professionals often shy away from the word "brand" thinking it artificial and manipulated, or only applicable to tins of beans and fancy footwear. However, the reality is that every person has a reputation – amongst their friends, family, work colleagues and clients. So, like it or not, you already have a reputation and by extension, a brand. In simple terms, your reputation is your own personal brand. This chapter looks at what reputation *you want to have* and then looks at how you can go about shaping that reputation into a strong and beneficial personal brand.

DEVELOPING YOUR BRAND – what reputation do you want to build for yourself? How can you use the techniques used by famous brands to build and maintain your own reputation?

Developing strong and mutually supportive relationships is at the heart of successful networking. There has been a tremendous amount of research since the 1980s examining how people relate to each other, what is happening in the brain, why we feel drawn towards some people and what makes for a lasting relationship. Starting with an understanding of what bonds people together in mutual support, we can then examine the latest research on what makes someone like you, how they assess if you are a help or a danger and how an understanding of the neuroscience behind much of human behaviour can guide you towards making and maintaining strong connections.

THE SCIENCE OF ATTRACTION – what makes someone like you? What is going on in the minds of people that you meet? Understanding the workings of the human mind will help you to build strong and resilient relationships.

The growth of online networking tools, particularly LinkedIn and Twitter, has transformed how professionals can network. Although these are essential tools, many people have avoided them or cannot see how they work. Just as often, professionals have started to use them, added a hundred or so connections but then are not sure what to do next.

In fact, online networking is without doubt one of the most powerful methods that you have. Even used on its own (without face to face networking time) this can be massively effective and provide an easy answer for an introvert professional, provided that you learn how to use online tools. Finally, the ability to progress your networking online in spare moments of downtime at your desk (or on your smartphone or tablet when on the move) makes this a great way of weaving networking into an already crowded professional life.

ONLINE NETWORKING – powerful, great for introverts and an ability to network in spare moments throughout the day, makes this the number one choice for many professional people.

Throughout this book, you will both find ways of building your network of connections and ways of being helpful to them. It is the opposite of the way that people typically think about a network. They want to build a network because they have all kinds of needs that they want to fulfil. They may want to find a job, develop new clients, build up their profile and so on. The only problem is that it can't be much fun meeting these people because they have so many things they want *from* you. Can't you tell when you meet someone like that? Typically these people come across as salesmen and saleswomen telling you about themselves and trotting out well prepared "elevator pitches".

So this is a chance to reflect upon the opposite approach and to look more deeply into how you can help other people and the (well researched) effects that this behaviour will have upon the people that you meet.

WHY HELPING OTHER PEOPLE WORKS – imagine that the worst thing that can happen to someone that you meet, is that you engage them in a pleasant conversation so that you can find ways that you might be able to help them and then offer that help.

It's as easy as that. At each stage you will see real life examples of what to do and what traps to avoid. We know that if we don't make the experience pleasant and achievable then it just won't work. So our system is based upon thousands of real life examples, showing clearly what works and what doesn't.

ONE

THE POWER OF FOCUS

Standing out in a competitive job market

Let's start with a story about Jess. Although she ended up completing her training as a lawyer, at a time when only around one in five were succeeding in gaining the required training contract in the UK, Jess took a somewhat meandering route. What she knew was that she was passionately interested in the environment and conservation. So much so, that it was while studying for her Masters of Science degree in Conservation that she decided that she was really interested in how governments and laws affected conservation issues. It was only at this point that Jess decided that she wanted to qualify as a lawyer who specialised in conservation.

Then she rather cleverly realised that she needed to start networking with potential employers straight away. First, she joined as many professional organisations (relevant to her chosen topic of conservation) as she could. She was pleasantly surprised to find that they welcomed student members – even to the extent that she represented them in a student capacity at some events (useful for her c.v.). She started meeting people and at the same time building her own profile and recognition with people who could be very important to her future success.

She discovered that these type of organisations often had limited funds but had many areas of research that they were interested in pursuing. So she managed to turn her required work for her master's degree dissertation into a sponsored piece of research for a professional body (also useful for the c.v.). This meant that she had access to all of the members of that association to meet and question in carrying out her research. So she managed both to network and to raise her own profile while carrying out her dissertation work. Her first tip about networking was this. She saw that a lot of the value in attending relevant meetings was in talking to people *before and after* those meetings, even though that wasn't really comfortable for her. (We will look at how this can be made much easier and more comfortable for you in Chapter 5).

From her various conversations with people she met, she discovered that most law firms relied heavily on Summer Interns for their choice of future employees – so her aim was to secure one of these positions. Of course, her genuine interest in conservation issues and the various organisations that she had joined made for a more interesting c.v.

So it's really no surprise that, based on genuine interests that she had, she was able to plan and then carry out a job hunting project. She asks, "What do you read about or spend time on when you are not working? " That's a good guide to where your real interests lay.

You cannot just focus on your career choice

Now let's look at a lecture theatre with 40 of the brightest Master's Degree students in the world. One entry qualification for the course is that students are fluent in at least three languages. It is the session on networking for business and the students are asked "what career do you want?" More than half of them say "Investment Banking" or "Business Consultants". That's the problem. How can you, *passionately*, want to be an "Investment Banker"? Isn't the attraction really just about big money salaries? About what you can take out of the employer, rather than about finding and following your passion? That's understandable when you are starting your career, but there is a better way, while keeping to your planned career.

The class then ran some exercises to seek out their passions and interests and tried again. The students saw the difference and Joost from Amsterdam came up with "Geothermal Energy". It turned out that he had just been an intern at an energy company that was exploring this ground-breaking new way of heating and cooling homes and offices using the differential temperatures that exist underground. Now, everyone in that class remembers Joost because this is such a distinctive interest. It also meant that it was *really* easy to show him how to use networking to follow his interest and to fast track his career. Even today, if anyone in that class comes across anything relating to Geothermal Energy they can email it to him and when they meet others with that interest they know to refer them to Joost. He stands out in people's minds, he has a real interest to which others can relate. He could still follow his career path of becoming an Investment Banker or a Management Consultant, but using his true passion would give him a better way in.

Let's look at some other examples. Adam is a very successful Venture Capitalist based in Silicon Valley. When asked for the secret of success he says "be obsessed, or hang around obsessed people". Obsessed people are following their passions. It doesn't really matter what those passions are, it is the intensity of interest that matters.

Another master's degree student on an MBA course, once we went beyond the formalities, confessed that her real passion was music, she wrote a really long email about how much it meant to her. The advice to her is to make sure she uses that passion in her career. It may not be as a performer, but there are many ways that you can be close to music through a career in the media, in recording companies or music technology. She had an easy "tag" because she had a passion that she could discuss and use to connect with others who felt the same way. This led to her focusing her career in accountancy around advising companies in the music and entertainment sector. How much more satisfying, enjoyable and successful her career is going to be, rather than just "being" an accountant and doing whatever work was passed to you!

Using shared interests

So you can still aspire to be an accountant, a lawyer, an investment banker, a brand strategist, in fact *any* profession. But you can't just stop there, because no matter how good your grades are, you are pretty similar to everyone else who aspires to the same end result.

It's exactly the same when you are much more advanced in your career. You can stop being like everyone else and give yourself a tremendous career advantage by combining your true passions with your profession. You may not be able to achieve the change instantly. But just telling everyone about your real interests and using networking to connect with those who share them, will bit by bit change your professional focus.

That is really one of the joys of effective networking. We find it easy to connect with people who share our interests – *"we like people who are like us"*. And they feel the same way about us too. So, *first find your passion*.

You might already know what this is. You might be in the process of narrowing it down. You don't have to make a once in a lifetime decision because your passions can change during the course of your career. The best approach is to jump in and see how it works out. Some people, and it can be at many different stages of their careers, are concerned that, by announcing some special area of interest, they close off and risk missing out on other opportunities. They are worried that they will pick something too narrow, it will not be a success, and they are set back in their career as a result. That's true to an extent, but our experience has been that the risks of *not* choosing an area of focus are much greater – because you are bland, undifferentiated (we will see the risks of that later when we look at personal brand) and just "ordinary". Think about the different attitude that you will bring to your career if you have managed to combine your passions into your day-job!

Let's examine the risks a little more, because choosing a focus will make an immense difference to your success in networking. Let's say that you choose healthy eating as your area of interest or that you want to concentrate on social justice in terms of criminal sentencing policies. Whatever you choose, this book will show you how easy it is to network your way within that topic. What is not easy is to be "an M&A specialist" or "a restructuring expert" or an "investment banker" – because these are just too broad for people to hook onto and remember you (or for you to have a clear networking path ahead).

You do not have to limit yourself to one area (having two very specific ones is quite common) but three is probably a maximum. Nor do you need to make lifelong choices. First, if a focus is not working for you, then you can drop it and choose another. Secondly, as you gain more life experiences, you may find other areas of interest. Ask your friends to help. Ask them to notice the topics of conversation that make you really animated. Think about how you can use those passionate interests as a route into your chosen professional career, or to give you a new lease life if you are already mid-career.

How do you find your passion?

If you need help considering possibilities then there are some useful resources online that can help you to think about this. There is a great article online by Maureen Anderson who runs a US based talk show called The Career Clinic entitled "5 Ways to Find Your Passion" and this explains how she came to be a talk show host. Interestingly, the journey is, quite often, not in a straight line. She went via journalism in a local paper and only after that did someone else suggest that she should be on the radio. Search and read the article to see how it worked for her.

Here are some ideas on how to uncover your passion and make this the focus for your career and your life:

- Think about what you would do for a living *if you were guaranteed you could not fail.* Be realistic but very ambitious. So don't choose "lifetime ruler of the world" but you could choose "CEO of my own organic foods business". You can be very ambitious because, in the next stage, you are going to look at what could be a useful first step or two along the way. So, you might think about a career in nutrition or working in a natural food company as a useful step towards being CEO of your own organic foods business. You might also want to think about what extra training would help you to prepare for your ultimate career choice.

- Don't worry if you can't fully analyse your passion, particularly if you are at an early stage in your career. It's better that you find some areas of "interest" and start playing with them, rather than agonising about making this exactly right.

- The most important point is really to *start now.* If you leave this it will stop you networking effectively – and you need to build your network now – not in the weeks before you really need help from a network.

- Have a really good think about what you read about or do "when you are off duty". What articles are you drawn towards, what books do you buy and what online discussions do you follow?

The British philosopher, Alan Watts, makes a passionate case for the importance of finding out your true interests and making them your career when he asks:-

"What would you do if money were no object? How would you really enjoy spending your life? … And when we finally got down to something which the individual says he really wants to do, I will say to him, you do that. And forget the money. Because if you say that getting the money is the most important thing, you will spend your life completely wasting your time. You'll be doing things you don't like doing, in order to go on living to go on doing things you don't like doing. Which is stupid."

It's a passionate and forceful argument for the value of following your passions and not following the herd (or what your parents wanted you to do!) Or try answering this question which is one we often pose to students. "If we told you that all careers were paid exactly the same amount of money, then what career would you choose to follow with that knowledge?"

People who uncover their passion and build a career around that, hardly feel like they are working, and their love for their subject shines through and inspires others. This passion is what enables you to be really good at your chosen career, to be successful and to be happy. It is really crucial to find out what makes you happy and use that in your career. People often get this equation the wrong way around. They think "Once I am successful in my career, then I will be happy". In fact it's the other way around. When you are happy, then you will be successful. Tapping into your passions and using these in your career is what really works. Or, to put it another way, think of something that is completely uninteresting to you, and then imagine devoting your whole career to that.

Don't forget "Geothermal Energy" because we are going to use this for the examples throughout the book!

TWO

TARGET

OK, so you chose Geothermal Energy as your passion and area of focus (what a co-incidence, we must introduce you to Joost). Let's use that as a useful, if quite obscure, example of a focus, so that we can see how to target people who are going to be useful to you in your new career.

At this early stage what you need is a feeling for the landscape around your area of focus so that you can start to narrow down a list of companies and people (if possible) that you would like to meet. Don't worry too much if you don't have a very clear hit list of people – this will improve as you move through the following stages.

Using your passion to find others

The very first step (because you may not know the details of the people that you need to know) is to make sure that you publicise your areas of focus. This means putting this high up in your profile on LinkedIn (see Chapter 9) and making sure that people you meet know about your interest in Geothermal Energy. There's a really good reason for this – at some point someone will say "If you are interested in Geothermal Energy, then you must meet my friend, as he's interested in that too". This type of gratuitous introduction cannot happen unless you talk about what you are interested in. You will be really surprised at how well this works. Telling people about your passions is a crucial step in successful networking.

Have a good search around the internet, look for relevant websites and, where possible, join in the conversation. Particularly strong places to look for industry discussions are LinkedIn (through the use of groups) and on Twitter – where we recommend following the relevant industry media and thought-leaders (who should all have a presence). Bear in mind that, particularly in the early stages of networking, you can just be seeking out likeminded individuals and learning from them. This is an area of focus, you don't yet need to be an expert in it. This type of early activity is important. It helps you to find out more about your topic, and joining in conversations online is a great way to start building your own profile.

It will also be useful to start searching in the following areas:

- To which news feeds / email updates on websites can you subscribe?

- What Google Alerts can you set up – use names of people, companies, issues, key words etc. (A Google Alert sends you regular news stories which contain key words that you have specified – if you are not sure how to set one up, just search on "Google Alerts" in Google for step by step instructions)

- What professional organisations can I join? Clubs, societies anywhere that you are going to meet likeminded individuals.

- Could you write an article on your topic or offer to give a talk to others?

Once again, let's embrace Geothermal Energy. How can you start to target relevant people? First, you can search in Google, Wikipedia and similar to find out the names of important companies and set up Google Alerts with those names. There might also be academics producing research papers and you can add their names and the names of key conference speakers to your Google Alerts.

Next you are going to join Groups in LinkedIn that cover Geothermal Energy (we look at this in more detail in Chapter 9). Joining these Groups means that you can see who else is active or of interest and start to follow them. Likewise in Twitter you can search on relevant hashtags and follow targets there.

Do not worry that you might need to cold call or approach people that you come across during this research phase on your own (and risk a pretty strong rejection). Our advice is that you should *never* cold call anyone because we know how annoying it is to receive such calls. The real benefit of networking comes later on, when your own network will arrange for a warm introduction for you. Not only is that the most effective method because it carries an implied recommendation from the introducer, but it also makes sure that you are not going to be on edge or nervous at a first meeting (because first impressions do count).

Where will you go?

It's at this stage you can also start thinking about where you will go in order to network with the right people. This is where the power of focus becomes really apparent. By choosing to concentrate on real passions of yours, it makes it easy to search out clubs and societies that you can join (if you are early on in your career, bear in mind that many have a separate student section) and to search online for upcoming events or to join in the conversation online on blogs, websites and LinkedIn.

THREE

FIRST CONTACT

There is a real and consistent concern that we come across when we raise the topic of having a first meeting with someone who is going to be relevant to your future. Why should anyone want to spend time with you, even more so if they are more senior or possibly in a position to give you a job or some valuable introductions? You know why you want to meet them and they may have worked that out too.

This worry is compounded by the fact that people who have power to give out work or spend budgets will typically be approached badly, regularly, by others who want jobs or money from them. A regular annoyance will be the absolutely awful cold call when someone in sales interrupts your day with a speech (always delivered at speed) about some great opportunity that they have or why they need a meeting. We can't think of anything less likely to get a positive response than a cold call.

So, given the absolutely awful way that these people are often approached, they may also be quite protective of their time. After all, it's not much fun being continually hit upon by people who want to sell you something or who want something from you. There are two lessons here. First there is timing (build relationships *before* you need them – don't try to build relationships when you really need them) and secondly, there are some real secrets involved in successful approaches. Ignore these and you won't just be unsuccessful, but you will also start to earn a reputation as someone to be avoided.

Building successful relationships

The first rule is to have a genuine interest in a topic or a person. Yet again this is where having a passion for Geothermal Energy is going to be so useful. Because you have decided that this is where you future is going to be, you can start to make contact with people who already work in the sector. The real power of networked introductions is going to come later, as you build up your contacts. But even at this early stage there are a number of great ways to initiate some contact.

Asking for advice

Business people are always happy to talk about their careers and their industry or profession – provided that they are approached in the right way. Asking for advice is a great way to make an approach and to make really clear that it is advice that you are looking for, not a job. So, for example an approach along the lines of "I am thinking of building a future in Geothermal Energy. I can see from [LinkedIn Groups] [an article in (trade journal)] [your speech at (industry conference)] that you are a recognised expert in this and it would be great if you could give me [10 minutes over the phone] [advice over a coffee] so that I make sure I set off in the right direction. I am currently [in year two of my Economics Degree] and so some insider advice at this stage in my career would be absolutely fantastic."

There is an element of asking for a real favour here, because you are asking someone to give up their time and people are generally busy. However flattery is always good ("I keep coming across your name as one of the experts in this field"; "I really enjoyed the article that you wrote in (trade magazine)" etc.) You really do have to be genuine about this. You must be both interested in their topic and *not* seeking a job from them. It will also make a big difference if you can have someone introduce you to this person. You can use LinkedIn for that (see Chapter 9) or you can use someone that you met through your face to face networking activities (covered in Chapter 5). Later on we are going to look at asking your connections to make introductions on your behalf which is in fact the main benefit of good networking.

But if you cannot arrange an introduction, then a polite email which also shows that you know something about them can be very successful. Just last year Kevin spent several hours both in meeting and corresponding with a Canadian author who contacted him to say that she was writing a book on a particular topic and "everyone keeps mentioning your name as the person I need to talk to." Suckered in by this relatively simple piece of flattery, Kevin subsequently wrote the summary that she asked for and which then made it as one of the Chapters in her book. So for the sake of just 12 pieces of flattery in emails, she had a book written for her! Similarly, the Financial Times Journalist, Lucy Kellaway, tells the story of how she ended up spending a huge amount of time travelling a very long way to give a talk to help a charity that she had never heard of before, because they started with some relatively mild and unimaginative flattery. (She called this technique "Superflattery" if you want to read the whole story then just search on that).

There is also some useful research on this. It's called "the Investment Effect" which means that if someone with value to give spends time helping you, then they will want to continue helping you because this reinforces their feeling that they did the right thing in the first place by giving up time to help you. We recently came across someone really senior using this – we agreed to leave him anonymous. He had just joined a new organisation and was making a point of visiting very senior people there and asking them "what advice would you give to someone like me, who has just joined". Clever, because he both received some great advice and was building up an investment effect that these people were likely to give him further help in the future, when he needed it.

In addition, both of us are extremely careful to make sure that we are polite, kind and attentive to receptionists, secretaries and PA's. Never, ever, underestimate the power and importance of these people. They are often "gatekeepers" and decide who gets through to see people in the organisation and who doesn't. When they have been helpful we make certain that we say thanks and even drop off a small gift. We would say that you can get in to see almost anyone in the world, if you first make a friend of their PA. We could give examples, but we decided it's best to keep this quiet!

Developing your voice - writing an article or running a blog

Apart from anything else, this shows the real interest you have in your passion and you will undoubtedly learn more about your subject as you write the article or update your blog. If you are going to write an article, bear in mind that you don't have to aim for the leading journal. Start at the bottom and look for opportunities to contribute a free article either to a magazine or online in someone else's blog or in a relevant website. The approach that you make to your target person is then just the same. You are writing an article and you would like their input. Give as many details and you can and in particular tell them why you want to talk to that person (for example you saw another article they had written or saw that they spoke at a conference on that topic etc.) Or you might start by following them on Twitter or finding out information through their public Profile in LinkedIn.

Meeting at an event

You can invite people that you want to meet to an event. That sounds really ambitious but it's really just a question of thinking of what you have that is of value to others. For example a group of law graduates in the US were worried about a tightening jobs market and wanted to avoid just receiving rejections by writing to firms that they didn't know, asking for jobs. They realised that law firms were not at all good at using social media like LinkedIn and Twitter to market themselves and to look for clients. So they organised their own event to teach lawyers how to make the most of online activity and invited partners from the local firms to come along as part of their University's "Outreach Program".

The result was that this was a great way for law graduates to meet partners in a really relaxed environment and to learn about what it was like inside a law firm. Connections made and a great opportunity for the students to follow up afterwards (by offering more help, for example offering to help a partner to create a great LinkedIn Profile, or use a Twitter account, or by asking for some advice).

Research

Carry out some research in your area of interest and then make contact with your targets to ask for help with the research. This has a lower rate of success with busy business people so you really need to target it properly. You need to compliment them – tell them why you chose to write to them – make it individual and not just a template email to all. Show them the value in the research and offer to send them a copy of the conclusions. Sales people often use "research" as a way in to clients so you need to emphasise that you are not selling and have nothing to sell. An additional benefit of research is that the results are often of real value in enabling you to write an article or in providing you with good insights that will be invaluable when you are approaching a target. An approach to an editor could be to say that you recently carried out a research project and you think that the results would be of interest to their readers. This is a pretty good way in. Once an editor has said yes then you can use the article as a great way in to other people, in fact you can ask the editor to suggest good people to contact for comments.

Whenever you do make contact with someone for research, ask them who else you should be talking to and then ask if they can make the introduction. This is a great way of finding influential people and being introduced to them!

Warm introductions

The very best way to meet anyone, is to arrange a warm introduction from someone that you already know – and that is where face to face networking (or the alternative for introverts shown in Chapter 5, if you hate doing that) is so useful. As you build your own network of connections you will find it much easier to ask for warm introductions. Once you have found someone that you would like to meet, talk to, or email, then finding a warm introduction to them is your number one priority – and also why building your own network of friends starting *now* is so crucial to your future success. Don't worry too much at this early stage that you are not able to obtain a warm introduction. The purpose of this chapter is to start you thinking about the people that you would like to meet (your targets) and to show you that even at an early stage there are relatively gentle ways to make contact.

You can think of your journey here a bit like Tarzan swinging his way through the trees to reach his destination in the jungle. You need a vine (your existing contact) to swing you across to the next tree – that's the person that you want to meet. But avoid dropping people once you have had what you wanted. Otherwise they will feel used. Stay in touch and look for an opportunity to return the favour.

Timing

You need to have your network in place and available to you when you need it. If you don't start early but you wait until you really need it (finding a job or changing jobs for example) you will find it much harder to both build and benefit from that network in a short space of time. Initial contact is just a way of starting this off, starting to build the business friendships that are going to be with you throughout your whole career. In the following chapters we are going to cover in more detail how you can make and nurture these important personal connections.

FOUR

FIRST IMPRESSIONS

What if we told you that you can be instantly more attractive, and that people that you meet will think that you are more intelligent, more successful and more likeable? All with almost no effort on your part. That would be worth having wouldn't it?

And what if we told you that there are "tricks" that you can use when you meet someone that will make them think that you are really interesting and that they want to see you again. Without your needing to be funny, clever or inspiring (all of which would take real effort wouldn't it?)

This chapter looks at the initial impact that you make when you meet people face to face – although a lot of the lessons also apply online. It really splits into two distinct areas – your demeanour (how you look and behave) and, quite separately, what you actually say. Then, in the next chapter, we are going to look at face to face networking skills – especially for those people who hate the idea of small talk and mixing with groups of strangers.

What do I look like?

Whenever you meet another person, your brain will be very rapidly forming a very clear impression of them – and this applies whether it's the first meeting or someone that you know well. Your brain will take in hundreds of pieces of information without you realising, building small observations up into hypotheses about this person you've just met. Have you ever seen someone that's made you uneasy and you can't figure out why? That's your brain spotting something out of the ordinary and flagging it up for the subconscious to have a closer look.

One of the biggest factors in what people are going to think about you is this – *are you smiling or not?* We have evolved to be socially primed towards people who are smiling. This means that you have at your disposal an easy way of making people think better of you – just smile and look happy. Try it for a few days. It will not feel particularly natural at first. We do mean *really smiling* and looking happy. The evidence is this:

- People will think that you are more attractive

- That you are more intelligent (!)

- That you are more competent (!)

In fact, smiling is something of a people magnet. It implies that you are happy, successful and easy to get along with. That's a lot of messaging to come from such a simple act. Think about the impression you create by looking serious. Unapproachable, defensive, not likeable. One law firm Managing Partner used to approach people who were looking serious and enquire, in a worried tone, "Is everything alright?" When the victim replied in the affirmative he would add "Well then you need to tell your face that!" Why was this important? Because if you walk around looking serious or miserable then that creates a pretty depressed atmosphere – it's contagious to your team and affects the work atmosphere.

Think about the effort made at really great hotels to welcome you with a broad smile as if they had been looking forward to your arrival all day. They do this because they know the impact that is going to have upon you. You will feel welcomed and liked even though all they did was greet you with a big smile. There is even evidence that – if you smile a lot – it actually makes you happier. Just exercising your muscles to smile affects your mood. People who make an effort to look happy actually are happier. How happy should you look? Our advice is to search online for an image of Jack Nicholson playing "The Joker" from the Batman films and then just dial it back a little from that. Yes just a little! Then try walking around happy all day and see the reaction that you receive. You are going to be surprised at how this changes people's reactions to you, and also how unnatural it feels to smile this much. But you can become used to it and our advice is that you should. As they say, "If you see someone without a smile, give them one of yours". Ok you can be sick now, but in any case try it.

To your surprise, you may find that, at least at first, walking around with a smile doesn't feel at all natural. It takes quite a bit of practice. And it can be a matter of "turning it up" as you meet people. The next story is a good example of that.

What *being happy* means in practice

John was a mid-ranking partner in a Big Four Accounting Firm when he was offered the opportunity to move from their regional office in Bristol to their UK Head Office in London. Should the whole family move? With a daughter happily settled into a great school in Bristol, and about to sit some very serious exams, John and wife Debbie decided that the worst thing they could do would be to disrupt their daughter's schooling.

So the solution was for John to live in a flat in London during the week, traveling there on Monday morning and then coming "home" for weekends on Thursday or Friday evening. At the time John had a great career coach called Tony. Tony said that it was absolutely crucial that, when John arrived home on Thursday or Friday evening, that he walked into his family home as an excited, happy, energetic person. Of course, after a week working in London and often travelling around the world it would have been much more natural for John to arrive home tired and deflated at the end of the week. Tony told John that he must never do that. If John felt tired, he had to park his car around the corner from home and make himself cheerful and happy – to force himself into a positive mood if need be.

Why? Because if John arrived home miserable at the end of every week that would have a terrible impact on the family. They had to cope all week with the extra work that came about because John wasn't there to help. If, when he did come home, he arrived miserable and exhausted then what would be the impact of that? Very soon his family would be dreading his return rather than antici-pating it. If John arrived happy and energetic then he would lift the mood, not depress it. John thought this was some of the best advice he had ever received. After all counselled Tony, "You wouldn't walk in to see a client looking tired and miserable – so why treat your own family worse than that. Put some effort into being an "up" person for them."

Interestingly, when we are presenting lectures or seminars, we watch people arriving and see that *most people* look pretty serious / miserable. Now, of course, that could be because they are not looking forward to seeing us, but hoping that was not the case, we looked at groups arriving for other events, just in case. It's the same. It looks like the default mood for most people is not very happy. In fact when we talk to these sad looking people we find that they are, in fact, per-fectly happy – they just had no idea that their face was not reflecting that fact. This phenomenon is widely recognised, it has been parodied as BRF (a "bitchy resting face") this just means that, at rest, your face looks miserable. Watch out for this as it creates a bad impression without you having to do or say anything!

How to choose the right dentist

Lesson – the biggest single impact you are going to have on people is whether you smile and look happy or not! Let's look at another actual example. Recently, Martin's dentist left town. He had been a patient of this dentist for more than 10 years and felt that he had quite a personal relationship with him. Martin first became a patient of James when he moved to London and decided it would be good to have a local dentist rather than relying on his original family dentist back in Manchester. Martin asked around and found James. He was a really nice guy and his practice was close to where Martin lived in London. It was only James' decision several years later to move and take his family into the countryside that meant that Martin had to find another dentist. As it happened Martin was due a check-up so just went back to his practice and the receptionist put Martin onto another dentist in that practice. Martin saw him, but found him to be very serious. He quickly decided that this was not the dentist for him. Let's be clear, Martin chose his dentist on "smile factor". Martin has no idea if this new dentist is a good or a bad dentist but instinctively knew that he did not want to be a patient of such a serious, miserable dentist. Professional people often underestimate the effect that smiling and being friendly has upon their clients. But most clients are looking for someone they can relate to, particularly if they may end up spending quite a bit of time with them.

Why do we, quite intuitively, want to work with people who are smiley and happy? Our theory, is that it's because happiness is not only contagious, but smiling people are visibly enjoying their work and that's a strong sign that they will do a good job for us. Think of service in a restaurant, how does a sullen server who doesn't smile leave you feeling? Are you confident they paid attention to your order and care? The same applies to how people see us.

Chemistry beats facts and figures

If you made a list of factors about how you distinguish between a good and a bad dentist it's pretty unlikely that you would put "friendly / smiling" at the top of the list. Isn't competence going to be number one? So it is interesting to see that when people come to make these decisions, they often make these choices of which professional to instruct largely based upon personal chemistry! Now there can be an exception if you need a really specialist professional advisor for a "life or death" matter. In those cases you simply want the best and will put up with a poor bedside manner. These experts can be "reassuringly arrogant" – the human equivalent of "reassuringly expensive". But, if you are *anything less* than that type of rare expert, smiling and being friendly is going to make a surprisingly big difference to your career. In fact, recent research in the U.S., found that doctors who had a friendly bedside manner were less likely to be sued by patients when things went wrong.

Do you look successful?

The second biggest impact is going to be how you look. What does that mean? Well, if you are at all ambitious, you need to "fake it until you make it", along the lines of the old advice "dress for the job you want, not the job you have" (unless of course the job you actually want is a WWE wrestler and you work in a formal office). This means that you should present as if you are already at the next stage in your career. We were always impressed by stories of David Bowie, who, as a penniless musician living in a squat, would save money so that he could arrive at an event in a limousine. He decided that if he was going to be a rock star, then he ought to start looking and behaving like a rock star. Sure enough, people who attended his early gigs and saw someone with all the trappings of a rock star who'd made it believed that's what Bowie was. There has been a lot of research on this, which says – *you are who you think you are.*

In fact, there is now some great research (carried out by Amy Cuddy at Harvard Business School) that not only do you hold yourself in a more confident position when you feel confident, but that the reverse is true as well – acting confidently, makes you feel more confident! This means that if you hold your body in a confident position (even just for two minutes) you will actually be more confident and behave more confidently. Let's look at this in a bit more detail. If you are nervous, sad or upset you shrink your body. You may touch your face. You close up. You make yourself smaller. If you are feeling very confident, powerful and successful you make yourself big.

Think of athletes punching the air when they cross the finish line first, how soccer players run around with their arms spread out when they score a goal. People who have been blind from birth and so have never seen this, also behave this way when they feel confident. This is "big body" behaviour. Look also at how politicians giving speeches are taught to spread their arms wide apart. All of these are primate signals of confidence and strength. Research has shown that just behaving in this "big body" way for two minutes gives you more confidence! Standing tall or spreading yourself across two chairs in a lecture room or standing up and leaning forward into a desk has an actual effect (increased levels of testosterone and reduced levels of cortisol – the stress hormone). This can be a great exercise to do before going into a stressful situation.

What you should start to understand is this – smiling and feeling confident has a real impact upon who you are, how you behave and what other people are going to think of you.

That is probably why we start our face to face networking training by asking people to make a list all of their worries so that we can deal with them one by one. If you going into a networking situation in a worried state of mind then it will affect the outcome. We are delighted to say that the overwhelming response, after the training, is that all of the worries were completely unjustified. Face-to-face networking may not be great fun for everyone (introverts in particular find making small talk very tiring) but it can certainly be made relatively easy. Most of the worries that people have about networking a room are based on a misunderstanding of the purpose of networking, or because they simply have never been taught how to do it the right way. In the next chapter we are going to deal with the skill of networking a room – and also explain how to network effectively without working a room, if it's really not for you.

FIVE

NETWORKING A ROOM

What could possibly go wrong?

What if we told you to go into a room of 200 people that you have never met before and successfully network with them? What is going through your mind? What are your worries? When we are teaching groups of people about face to face networking skills and ask them for their worries, the list would typically include the following:

- I might be left on my own with no one to talk to - while everyone else in the room is happily engaged in animated group conversations. Being the only person in the room who is on your own is a terrible feeling!

- If I start talking to someone I don't know what to say to them.

- I might be stuck talking to only one person all night because I don't know how to end the conversation and break away.

- I'm worried that the conversation will just dry up.

- I don't know how to join a group of people.

- I forget people's names and then somebody else comes up and I cannot introduce them.

- I might end up talking to somebody senior, and why would they want to talk to me? I don't know what to say to them.

- I am not sure what to do about business cards. Am I supposed to offer mine, or ask for one?

The vast majority of people attend networking events very ineffectively and endure quite a lot of wear and tear on their emotions, energy and time as a result. That is both surprising and annoying given that it is really easy to learn how to network well. That is the purpose of this chapter. You do not have to perform face-to-face networking if it is a nightmare worry for you, and later on in this chapter we are going to look at networking for people who hate networking. That's because there are other, perfectly effective ways, of being a great networker without ever walking into a room of 200 (or more) people you don't know. However, before you skip to that, it's worth re-examining face-to-face networking to demystify it and take the worry out of it, just in case you find yourself in a position where you need the skills. Before we do that, let's look at the real purpose of networking. We think that it will surprise you.

Why are you networking?

When we ask people why they need to network, they give exactly the types of reasons that we would have given when we started to do this. Typical reasons as follows: –

- I will meet people who can offer me a job.

- I will meet people who can become clients of mine in the future.

- It will raise my profile so that more people will know me.

- I will meet people who will become good friends of mine.

- By speaking to people in my chosen area of interest, I will gain greater knowledge about that.

- I can become better connected internationally.

- To find mentors.

- To meet friends and partners (business and personal)

- I can create new possibilities by meeting new people and thinking about what we could do together – so that I can find work without going through the typical job application process.

The problem with this – and as a result the problem with almost all networking training that we have seen – *is that it is all about YOU!* In fact, we are not sure that we would want to meet you at a networking event because you are so greedy for all the opportunities that you can see coming from us. It can be even worse when the person you meet actually has the power to give you these things – such as a job or a client assignment because it can become very awkward if you move into "sell mode" about how great you are and how wonderful it would be for them to have the benefit of working with you. We have seen lots of training around "elevator pitches" but such a pitch has a substantial risk of being a "sell". (An elevator pitch is a brief way of introducing yourself – and can be delivered in the time it takes for an elevator to move between floors. We will look at this later on). There is room for elevator pitches, they can be very handy to bring clarity to your thoughts – but they are not a good way to build rapport with others.

In fact, we think that a lot of the worry and stress that we had when first networking with people, was that we felt under a huge obligation to impress them in some way so that they would want to see us again. The pressure became even more intense if we were asked to see "important people" who might be clients of our employers already, or could be particularly valuable in terms of our own future.

It was many, many years before we realised two things – first, the purpose of networking was not to deliver the long list of wants that we had, and secondly that there was a very easy way of talking to people which was relaxed and pleasant for both of us, would not involve us having to sell or impress them in any way and nevertheless would leave them with a very good impression of us.

There are two very important rules.

Rule Number One: the purpose of networking is to meet *relevant people* and to *help them*.

We really cannot emphasise this too much. "Relevant people" comes from the focus that you have – from your passions. Relevant people are those with the same interest or who can help you to achieve your aims. That's why focus is so important – without that you cannot know whom you would like to meet. The next breakthrough is that you are not expecting these relevant people to help you – on the contrary all you are going to do is try to think of ways that you could *help them* (immediately or at some future time).

Rule Number Two: there is a very easy way to talk to people that will impress them and make them like you.

The second lesson is good news too – you don't need to have some brilliant outgoing personality, a vast stock of knowledge or the level of humour typical of a stand-up comedian in order to talk to the people that you meet, and to create a good impression with them. In fact trying to behave like that is both very pressuring for you and pretty certain to fail. The good news is that there are really simple techniques to use when talking to other people that can be learnt in minutes, are easy to perform and will definitely create a good impression with them.

Now that we have two golden rules, let's look at the practical side.

The physical aspects of networking a room.

Once you have thoroughly absorbed these two rules we can move on to looking at the actual mechanics of networking a room in a way that will not stress you out. After all, the worst that can happen now to any person that you meet is that you might help them!

Removing the worries.

When you analyse the typical worries that people have they split down into two separate areas. There are issues around the physicality of networking in room (breaking into groups, getting away) and then quite separately there are issues about what is going to be said. Let's look at each of these areas in turn.

Entering groups.

Next time that you enter a room where people are networking, you need to look at whether they are in either "closed" or "open" groups. You can see examples of this set out below for two, three or four people (the actual number is irrelevant). In a closed group people stand face to face or in a clearly closed circle. An open group, on the other hand, has left a very clear gap allowing others to join them. This is a really crucial distinction and having looked at the pictures you will find that the next time you enter a room full of people will see that they very definitely are formed into open and closed groups. At worst, it might mean walking in to find that everybody is in a closed group. Our advice is simply this. You can walk up to any open group, say hello and join the group. Open groups are signalling that they are happy for other people to join them. Later on, we will look at what you say to them when you join, but in practice it doesn't really matter because *anything will do*. We will give several examples later on that you will find really easy to use.

Let's look at this one group at a time. Two people can either form an open group (standing more side by side) or they can be closed – face to face. Look at Picture 1 as you need to understand this properly:

CLOSED   OPEN

Picture 1

On the left you can see a closed group of two people. They are standing facing each other, eye to eye. Leave them alone. A closed group is just that, closed! Incidentally this works both in finding good business connections and in dating as well. If you start talking to one person and you want to hold onto them and keep others away then just turn your body so that you are face to face with them – forming a closed group. If they open the group back up by moving their body then that is not a good sign. But if they stay closed with you then that is a sign of interest.

In the second group of two in Picture 1, there is an open edge and this is signalling (consciously or unconsciously) that they are happy for others to join their group and talk to them. Here you can just walk up to the open group and say hello – it really doesn't matter what you say initially – honestly *anything will do.* You could say "Hello do you mind if I join you?" or you could say "Hi. My name is David. What brought you to this event?" or "Hello. My name is Mike and I am studying at University College. Where are you from?" Later on we are going to look at how to manage a great conversation, how to really engage with anyone in a way that they will enjoy. For now it's just about opening lines and joining in and the great news is that anything that starts with you saying hello is fine.

Now let's try that with three people:

CLOSED   OPEN

Picture 2

Now you see it, it's quite obvious isn't it? An open group – whether it's two, three, four or more is easy to just walk up to and join in. So this is really just about reading body language and positioning.

Now let's try that with four people and see how that looks. The next time that you walk into any networking situations you can look around and you will start to notice that there are only three possible combinations – closed groups, open groups and people who are on their own (we will look at the solos later on).

CLOSED   OPEN

Picture 3

Our advice for closed groups is simply this – leave them alone unless you actually know one of the people in it really well and they can join you into the group. By definition, a closed group will be busy discussing something that is of interest to all of them, and by closing the group into a circle they have indicated that they are not looking for other people to join in.

Leave closed groups alone

Why do we say to people that if they come across a closed group they should leave them alone? This is based upon a real experience that Kevin had early on in his career. He persuaded his firm to join the British American Chamber of Commerce. Although it cost a lot of money, there was an extremely good reason for this. He thought that if he networked within this organisation then he was very likely to meet Americans and that could well lead to him having free trips to America paid for by the firm. This was definitely very strategic (at least on his part, if not on the part of his firm). Shortly after joining the Chamber, he attended his first event which was a dinner being held at the Grosvenor House Hotel in London's Park Lane. It was a formal dinner and he arrived dressed up in his dinner jacket to enter a room in which there were at least 1000 people all of whom were busily engaged in animated conversation in closed groups. He could not see a way in to join any group.

This immediately felt very awkward, because there is nothing worse than being the only person on your own in a room where 1000 other people are all in groups and having a great time. He now had a choice to make. He could go back home, but then he faced the problem that he would have to admit to his work colleagues in the morning that, although he had gone to the networking event, he had been too frightened to talk to anyone. That felt like quite an embarrassing admission to make.

The alternative was that he had to break into one of the groups and start talking. He decided that this was scary, but this was what he was going to do. Right next to him, where he had entered the room, was a group of six people. Kevin hovered close to them for a while hoping that somebody might notice and ask him to join the group, but they did not. So in the end, he touched one of the members of the group on the shoulder and when that person turned around Kevin asked him if could join the group because he was a new member of the British American Chamber of Commerce and this was his first event.

People at networking events are polite. There was no problem at all and Kevin was quickly introduced to all the other people in the circle. It turned out that they were all from Citibank (as it was then called). After those introductions the group then went back to the conversation that they had been having before he had interrupted them. This conversation was about George. They had all worked with George from many years and he had dropped down dead last week so they were all telling their stories, some amusing, some heartfelt, about what it had been like to work with him and what a character he had been.

Kevin quickly realised something. Without having the advantage of actually knowing or working with George, it was going to be pretty difficult for him to join in with this conversation! He decided that he needed to leave, but as he only just joined the group this seemed pretty embarrassing as well. Kevin hung on for a few minutes listening to stories and then pretended to have seen somebody that he knew across the other side of the room that he had promised to meet and he made his excuses and left. Luckily, everyone was then called in to dinner and so Kevin went to his allocated seat hoping it would not be on the Citibank table.

How to make sure that you are never locked out

This was such an awkward experience for Kevin that he decided that he did not want to have this happen ever again. After some thought, he realised that he had made the classic professionals' mistake of running late. By being one of the last to arrive at a networking event it will inevitably mean that people who have been going to the event for many years have already met their friends and are talking to them in closed groups. But there is a relatively easy way of avoiding this *ever* happening to you.

Just make sure that you are one of the first people at any networking event. In fact, there are a number of benefits to being early. At the quiet time at the start of the event you have a chance to chat to the people who have organised the badges and are setting them out on a table. You can ask about who else is coming and on many occasions the "badge managers" have been happy to arrange an introduction to someone we wanted to meet. If you spot someone's badge that you want to meet, you can just say "I would really like to meet [this person] – could you bring them over to me when they arrive?" – and they do! They want their networking event to be successful, so they are always willing to help their attendees benefit from the event and are therefore great allies of yours. Another benefit of arriving early is "singles" – people who are on their own at the event. As we are going to see, *singles are yours* and are one of the best and easiest parts of networking a room

Singles

There is something extremely awkward about being on your own at a networking event. Look around you the next time that you are in a roomful of people. Standing on your own means that you have no friends and that no one wants to talk to you. It's as simple as that! It is so embarrassing that people caught on their own immediately become very interested in their smart phones or in some papers they are carrying because it's not that they are stuck on their own it's just that *they have something else that is really important that they have to attend to and that is why they have chosen to stand on their own for a moment!*

If, like us, you have arrived really early at the networking event, then you are going to see single people arriving, or just standing on their own. They are yours. They belong to you! Why – because you can walk up to any single person and tell them your name and start with some very innocuous opening line like "Hello, I'm Alexis, can I introduce myself?" *It really doesn't matter what you say.* The reason is this – if someone is on their own at an event, then any smiling person walking up to them (you did remember about smiling didn't you?) to introduce themselves is the most welcome sight in the world because *it stops them being on their own!* This really works. It is so easy. You can simply arrive early and hover by the coffee. Then anyone coming off the coffee who is a single, you approach and say hello and, for example, ask them "what brought you to this event?" or, having looked at their badge and seen the name of the company that they work for, you might say "tell me what it is like working for [The Mafia]?" or whatever company it is that they are employed by.

Later on, we will look in detail at how to talk to people – for now we are just looking at some easy opening lines. After many years of experience in networking situations, we can say that spotting and approaching singles is one of the best things that you can do at a networking event. One of our American friends who watched us doing this described our behaviour as "acting like the Mayor's wife" – which we are, perhaps hopefully, assuming is a compliment. What we do is this - once we have approached our first single, we stay on the lookout for others, and as soon as we see one, we say to the person we are currently talking to, "that person over there looks like they are on their own, let's ask them to join us" until we have a crowd of about 10 (single) people that we have gathered up and introduced to each other. We kind of behaved as if we were hosting the event rather than just being attendees. We "hoovered up" every "single" in the room! We made a great thing of having everybody introduce themselves to each new joiner as that helped us remember everyone's names (more on that later).

Getting away

Sometimes, as soon as you say hello to someone, you realise that you don't want to talk to them. For example they may be someone working in a competitor organisation (who is also there to network) or you might decide that they are not for you on this occasion. In those circumstances we think it's OK to disengage straight away by smiling and saying something like "I'd better not tie you up" and then walking away.

More commonly, you have been talking to someone at a networking event, it's been fine, but you need to move on because the purpose of going to the event was to network and you want to make sure you didn't just meet one person. How can you bring the conversation to a close, bearing in mind the reality is that you are "dumping" this person so that you can meet some others. One expression that you could use would be, "Well, I had better not monopolise you, I had better let you circulate." What you are implying with this wording is – "you are the most interesting person here, everyone else here is absolutely dying to meet you, and here I am selfishly tying you up and keeping you to myself". So it is a way to end a conversation on a high. A fantastic trainer called Ian Redmond (look him up – Explore Training) teaches the phrase, "It's been great talking to you, I would like to stay in touch, do you have a business card?" He added that once they gave him a business card, they typically then asked for his. If you are at an early stage in your career and don't have business cards then have some printed so you have something to swap. It would be just as effective to say "It's been great meeting you, I'd like to stay in touch - can I connect to you on LinkedIn?"

What else can you do to disengage? Students often suggest going to fetch another drink or going to the toilet. The problem with the drink option is that the person you are talking to may also want another drink so may come with you. It is right that you will often find others at the drinks queue, so you may be able to join them into a conversation and then slip away, but it carries some risks. Presumably, the other person is rather less likely to follow you into the toilet, but then how many times in an evening can you disappear into the toilets without drawing attention to yourself?

A reasonably good option is to join another person into your conversation – so if you feel that you are "stuck" with someone, you can look out for a single –

suggest that you join that person into the group and then, after the introductions, you can just move on by saying "well, I had better circulate" and leaving them to it.

You can worry too much about this. It is fine to disengage at a networking event, because the other person also attended the event to network as well. As Kevin's wife explained to him, "maybe they were glad to get away too!" That had never occurred to him, as he had assumed that anyone who was talking to him would be devastated at his breaking away to talk to others, but there is a slim possibility that she was right.

In any event, you will soon start to learn that no one dies at networking events and very few are seriously injured, so it is OK to go networking and practice your skills. In addition, if you meet someone that you think is particularly interesting and *relevant* for you early on at an event, it is fine to be "stuck" with them for the whole event. You don't always need to circulate – it's a quality game, much more than it is about quantity.

Business Card Etiquette

Worth mentioning, because it is possible to do this badly. Quite often when you are at a networking event you will come across "vultures" – people who are there to sell things and are just looking for victims. These people always want to collect business cards (and give out their own) and it seems to be a numbers game for them. One memorable example of this occurred at a networking event organised at the offices of a Big Four accounting firm. There was a talk at 4pm on a topic that was of real interest, and this was followed at 6pm by drinks and canapés for networking. It was a well-attended event and about 60 or so people stayed on afterwards to mingle. About 15 minutes into this, our hero arrives and sees everyone spread around the room in 8 or so clusters of people (some closed groups, some open).

Starting nearest the door, he introduced himself as the senior "Restructuring Partner" and proceeded to give the group a mini lecture about all of the great work he had carried out in the last 12 months and then said "Well I'd better give you a card so you can contact me" and proceeded to hand each member of the group his card which everyone solemnly put in their pockets having made a mental note to avoid this idiot in future at all costs. In fact, without exception, as our hero left each group (having given them a 5 minute "drinking from a fire-hose" session about himself) everyone broke into a broad smile with a shared appreciation of how awful this was. Our hero returned to his office no doubt pleased with himself – he hadn't needed to sit through the seminar, and in less than an hour he had impressed 60 people and given out 60 business cards!

So, our starting position is this – we don't really want to give a stranger a business card because it has our phone number on it and the stranger may start phoning to sell us stuff. Secondly, why on earth would you need the stranger's business card – what use is that? At such an early stage you may need convincing that you want to stay in touch at all.

So, for us the key message is "not too fast". It's just like dating. If you meet someone you like for the first time, isn't it a bit pushy to ask for that person's email address and phone number? So we think it's important that you do this right, or you are going to create the wrong impression. Remember Rule Number 1: Networking is meeting relevant people and *helping them*. So it is only acceptable to ask for a business card if it is so that you can send them something of real value to them.

Do you need a business card? Perhaps you are still studying at University. Our advice would be to get some cards printed so that you have something to swap! There is a courtesy issue here – if someone gives you their business card then they may ask for yours in return. Even if it is just so they can easily remember your name when you make contact, it's handy to have something to leave behind.

Bear in mind also that there is a quite different business card etiquette in Asia where people will offer their card, held in both hands, at the start of a conversation. You should take and examine their card, ideally commenting upon their job title, location or company to show them that you have studied the card. You can then offer your card in return.

Starting to help

In Chapter 10 we will look at reciprocity, and how you can help other people, at this stage we would like to tell you about a game we play when we meet people for the first time. It is to ask questions that will help us to find out about *their* interests and then think about whether we have anything that would interest them. An article, a book, information on an upcoming conference, an introduction to someone that it would be useful for them to meet. This is with a view to seeing if they ask for details of the article, book, conference or introduction that we will have mentioned and then we can ask for their card so that we have an email address in order to send details. If done well, this results in the other person offering their card because they are keen for us to send them the information that could help them. So our game in this. Rather than *us* having to ask for *their* card, we want to create the situation where we have flagged up something useful we could give them, so that they actually offer us their card (or contact details).

So imagine that you start talking to someone and you move the conversation onto whether Twitter is a useful professional tool or whether it's just for fun. You do this because you came across a great article on this recently or because you read a fantastic book (called "Natural Networking") or something similar. Now, the person you are talking to, may have doubts about Twitter – in which case you could say "Actually I read a great article / book about Twitter that showed the quite surprising ways it could be used in business – would you like details / for me to send you the link to it?" Once they say yes then you need their email address.

If your entire focus is upon "how can I help this person" then you will find that you will collect business cards. Even if they do not offer you their card (or email address) remember that if you had a good conversation with someone but now need to move on then you can do that by saying "It was great talking to you and I'd like to stay in touch, do you have a business card?"

Here is an important tip – once you are given someone's business card you must actually look at it and read it (sometimes there will be something interesting to comment upon on the card). It is perceived as being really rude just to put it in your pocket without reading it. Quite often there might be something different about the card (a strong visual image, for example) and it is good practice to comment on that to show that you have read the card, or to notice the City where they work, etc. Very importantly, you need to write on the back of the card what you were talking about with this person. Don't do it in front of them (it looks a bit calculating) but as soon as you have broken away make notes about what you were talking about with this person and any follow up you have agreed with them (like sending them a copy article that you referred to in your conversation). If you didn't receive a card from them, it's useful to be carrying a sheet of paper with you that you can use to capture key information.

The reason this is important is twofold. First, you need to follow up on any offers of help that you made. Secondly, at the end of an evening you may well have 4 or 5 business cards in your pocket and *you will not remember who was talking about what, or what follow up you promised!* So it's crucial that you make notes so you can remember. There is a timing issue too – you need to send any promised follow ups the next day – this creates a great impression that you are on the ball – you action things fast. Just delaying by even a day so that you follow up two days later, has a much lesser impact.

Juggling

Unless you have been circus trained, holding a plate of food, eating, holding a drink and shaking hands at the same time is something of a challenge. There is an easy solution to this. Eat before you go (this makes a big difference). You should always have something to eat before any networking event in order to avoid any form of eating while standing up.

It means that you will be fuelled up, will not be distracted by the food and will have your hands completely free. You can hold a drink, but if it is alcohol then you need to drink really slowly – being drunk while meeting new people is not a great recipe for success. It is completely different from going out with an established friend and having one too many.

You will be much more relaxed at these events knowing that you will not have to juggle, can easily shake hands with anyone you meet and are not feeling hungry.

Remembering names

For some reason, when you are introduced to someone and they tell you their name, your brain immediately says "well you won't be needing that piece of information ever again" and wipes it from memory completely. There have been various research projects carried out on this, because it turns out that forgetting people's names is entirely typical. One theory that we like is that your brain, upon meeting anyone new, decides to give priority to visual memory and scans this person's face just like an electronic scanner would scan a photograph of a face. This takes a lot of processing power and so, for just a second or two, your brain is 100% utilised on the scan and literally cannot hear.

What we have found, is that unless you have some natural skill at remembering names, you have to start using techniques to help you to remember them. Here are several that we use:

- Ask them to repeat it. Just say "I'm sorry I didn't catch that, what was your name again." Bearing in mind everyone is as bad as you are at remembering names, they will be fine about having to repeat it to you.

- Say their name out loud – and ideally several times. For some reason this helps to implant it in your brain. So, after you have been told that someone is called Luke Warwick, you need to say "Luke it's good to meet you. I have a brother in law called Luke. So tell me something about [where you work]." Then when someone else joins the group make a point of introducing your new friend, "This is Luke. Luke works for [company] and was talking about their recent office move." What you should be trying to do is use their name as much as possible in those first few minutes.

- Try to make a picture out of their name and superimpose it on their face, in your mind. So you could put a picture of your brother in law's face (if he is called Luke!) on top of this Luke's face and you might build a castle and sit it on his head like a crown (after Warwick Castle). The more obscure, surprising, vivid or ridiculous the better.

Why does this matter? Because the sweetest sound that anyone will hear is their own name. Remember being at a crowded party and hearing your name being used right across the other side of the room? You picked it out of all the background noise. So we have very pleasant associations from our name and anyone who uses it a lot creates a great impression. We are hugely impressed when someone that we have only met once or twice before walks up to us and greets us by name. So the better that you become at remembering peoples' names, the better impression you will create.

Another helpful resource is LinkedIn – quite often when you are attending an event you can obtain a list of people attending in advance. You should always ask because it is often not provided automatically. You can then look through the list at any people that you met before and refresh your memory on what they look like by seeing their profile in LinkedIn – if you have connected to them after the previous meeting then their photo will be visible.

Belinda is one of the world's top Marketing Directors. She stayed recently at a wonderful five star hotel in Dubai. She was particularly impressed that the two receptionists at the business lounge always greeted her by name whenever she walked towards them from the lift. One evening, while she was sitting in the lounge, she looked across to the reception desk and saw that one of the staff was spending all his free time looking through the scanned passports of everyone on the business floors and memorising their names and pictures. How incredible is that? When Belinda checked in, they had taken a scan of her passport onto their computer system so they had a record of the picture and name of every guest. Then the receptionists spent any quiet time that they had studying the passport photos of the guests so that they could remember, and greet each guest, with their names.

We all have a similar system available to us now – using LinkedIn – which we will look at in Chapter 9.

Badge management

There may well be times when it is your event and you have organised the badges. There are some tips here that can make networking much easier. First, you can put a coloured stripe across the bottom of every badge that matches a coloured stripe on your badge. So, if you are particularly interested in the Technology Sector and you are hosting a mixed event then you can put a bright blue stripe (just use a felt tip pen) across the badges of all the attendees from that sector. That way, even across the far side of a room, you can spot people that you want to meet. It is fine also to explain this to people as you walk up to them – "I just wanted to say hello, because we have matching stripes. That means you are in the Technology Sector, like me. Tell me what's going on at the moment in [your company]."

Alternatively, if you want to allocate guests to hosts, then you can do that with coloured badges (or just different coloured felt tip stripes as above). We were most impressed when attending an event recently, to see this in action. When a guest arrived at the desk, they would be told – "Oh, I see you have a blue badge. That means that you are in Robert's group. Then you would be led over to a group of five people at coffee, in the middle of which was Robert (the host). He duly introduced each new guest to the rest of the group, all of whom stayed together throughout the seminar. It meant that no guest was ever left standing on their own and had a ready-made group of people to talk to, and to network with, throughout the day.

And if you hate face to face networking?

Quite a lot of people hate the idea of networking a room or a conference. They hate making small talk, find it both tiring and difficult to meet a stream of new people and they don't like the thought of attending big events. This is very typical introvert behaviour and very many great professionals are introverts. In fact for some work types it "comes with the territory" – to be good at your chosen career you are very likely an introvert. The worst thing that these people can do is to force themselves to network face to face at big events. They won't enjoy it and they are unlikely to be very good at it.

Fortunately, that doesn't matter because several of the most successful networkers we know are introverts and would probably hate being described as "great networkers". There is a really simple work-around that we discovered when attending a conference with a serious introvert who contrasted perfectly with an extreme extrovert. They both had a great conference but it is interesting to see the completely different techniques that they used.

The Conference was taking place in San Diego in the United States and would have more than 3,000 people attending. When first told about the conference the extrovert thought "that's great, I wonder who I will meet there." She attended the working sessions and stood at the back of the room and deliberately held back from sitting down until she saw somebody sit down (with a space next to them) whom she considered looked senior or interesting. Even better if she could see a slot where she would sit between two such people because she could introduce herself to both of them as she sat down (and introduce them to each other – helping all the time!) So she put some thought into where she sat at each of the many working sessions.

She put the same thought into lunches (pick a table that's about half full so she can see several people to talk to) and of course she was actively "working the room" at coffee breaks and drinks. She had a great time and met lots of interesting people. Luck was involved however. For example, she might sit down to lunch and find that she was sat next to a major competitor, so that wasn't likely to be a terribly useful source of future opportunities. She just accepted that some were really good and some were not. If she achieved one in three as useful contacts for the future she would think that this was pretty good – after all you may have to kiss a lot of frogs before one turns into your prince.

Overall she would say that she had a pretty good (if very tiring) three days at the conference. Lots to follow up, some good connections made and friendships started.

How introverts network

Her introvert colleague had a good conference too, but in a completely different way. Being somewhat more organised than she was, he had spent the two months leading up to the conference contacting all of his existing connections to find out who was going. As an introvert he had, quite typically, emailed his connections and had fixed *timed one to one meetings* with each of them. For example, he was going to eat breakfast in the conference hotel anyway, so he arranged to meet one of his contacts for breakfast. Likewise he had scheduled a meeting in every coffee break, lunch and dinner. These were not just his direct contacts – for a few of these he had asked existing clients if they could introduce him to someone he had wanted to meet but didn't know, and then they had all three sat together. His networking *was a series of one to one meetings*. Brilliant. He had met many fewer people than his extrovert colleague, but his were more targeted. Moreover, he was very comfortable and good at these one to one meetings – it was what he did well. *This is the secret of networking for introverts* and others who hate networking – pre-arrange one to one meetings (or maybe one on two if one of the others is a well-established contact already). Online networking tools are particularly useful for this as we will see in Chapter 9 – they make it really easy to find people worth meeting at any event (or City) that you are visiting. Bear in mind that this is not just about introverts meeting people that they already know – they find it just as easy to ask existing contacts to introduce them to someone new and we will look, later on, at how and why this works (why on earth someone you know would do this for you).

The extrovert colleague, after learning how well this introvert had done at the conference reflected upon this, and decided that his structured system was better than hers and that at the very next conference she would copy his methods. Of course, despite this good intention, she didn't, because that would have involved a degree of pre-planning and organisation that she did not have. This approach did not play well to her more spontaneous (less organised) personality. Not to worry – her system had an element of luck, of serendipity, where she would meet someone useful that she hadn't even thought about. Which is true and rationalised her different approach.

The important lesson here is to find your own style. If you are able to "work a room" then this is a useful skill – and it will improve with practice. But if that's not for you, or you try it out and don't feel you are getting enough out of it, then it is entirely possible to network in other ways – particularly by fixing one to one meetings and using LinkedIn and other online methods that we are going to describe later on. Introverts are, typically, very organised and so have a much greater chance of being able to organise one to one meetings ahead of an event. And they are also great listeners – so are very likely to have a productive meeting – more so than any extrovert.

What to say?

Whether you network a room or meet one to one, the most important issue is going to be what you say, after you have said hello. Let's look at that now in the next chapter.

SIX

MAKING AN IMPACT

(Includes the secret of universal attraction)

The challenge of the professional

Professional people, when they start networking, carry quite a burden – that of making sure that the interactions that they have with the people that they are going to meet are really successful. After all, who wants to meet someone only to find that the talk is slow, uncomfortable or leaves a bad impression. A very typical approach that this causes would be:

- I have just met this person who may be important to my future. They might offer me a job, send me future work or recommend me to others.

- I only have a limited amount of time in front of this person in which to make a real impact and leave them with a great impression of me.

- In order to do that I must reel off details of my achievements as soon as I can because only in that way can they judge me.

- I want them to want to meet me again so I need to be clever, funny, impressive, expert / all of the above.

This type of thinking puts you under real pressure. The more important the person that you meet, the more pressure you are under. This makes for really bad meetings in networking situations – remember the Big Four Restructuring Partner in the previous Chapter. He was 100% wrong. (You don't win any points for that unfortunately).

Here are the essentials for a great networking conversation:

- Talk about them, not about you. Be interested in them and ask good questions.

- Look for things that you have in common with the other person, create empathy around shared interests.

- Your guiding principle is that you are talking to this person in case *you can find ways that you could help them.*

- So the longer and deeper the conversation you have, the more chances that you will find that you have things in common and that there are ways you could help them.

That's the real key to our approach. There should be no pressure upon you. You are just going to talk to another person and have them talk about themselves and the maximum follow up might be that you have found something that could be of value to them, that you can give them for free. It is the opposite of sales. No one will regret meeting you. Let's look at this in much more detail.

Being interested, not interesting

To be genuinely interested in someone, in what they have to say, their opinions and experiences is both pleasurable and flattering for them. People like to talk about themselves and your enabling them to do that will make them really like you. So your first point of understanding is that you do not need to talk about yourself – why – because that is *not interesting to anyone other than you!* If you observe someone who is really boring you will find that all they do is talk endlessly about themselves. We used to call it the "I" count when we came across this in business – see how many times a person uses the word "I" in each minute. The more "I's" the more boring they are. It's the same with any Facebook feed that has endless self-pictures or endless details about everything that they are doing.

Your role is to have the other person talk about themselves in three ways (there is a hierarchy and you typically have to go from one to another, in order, as you start to know someone better). The order is usually

- The company

- Their role in the company

- Their own future (which may or may not be with that company)

Let's look at this in practice. If you meet someone for the first time who works for Coca Cola Corporation then you might say:

"Glad to meet the person who keeps me and my sister happy on Diet Coke. Tell me, what happens in a recession to soft drinks, do you suffer like everyone else or are you immune?"

Let's look at the wording in detail. If you have any connection to the company of the person to whom you are talking, then you should mention it straight away. Here, both you and your sister drink a lot of Diet Coke so it's a great tag line to say that. If you can say something positive about them then do. Then you can ask "how's business" but as that is such a boring question, you should dress it up a bit. All that you really want to do is to have them talk about what life is like for them in their company at the moment.

What if they respond with something like this? – "Well, we are not immune. There can be lower demand and pressure on prices. We have found that there are some areas of the world where we still have unsatisfied demand and great potential for us, so that means that we have shifted some of our focus to those countries."

What's you next move? It's to dig deeper – so for example, you might say "That's interesting, what has that meant for your role in the company?" or "Really, so what are some of the most interesting new markets for you in the world?" The crucial point is that you are not going onto some other question on another topic but are really digging around based upon their answer. That helps to stop it being like an interrogation.

They say "Well we have just announced that we are going to establish a new subsidiary in [country] and I need to learn all the rules of doing business there, as fast as I can."

In which case you might say "I think I know someone who set up business there about two years ago. If you would like to chat to them about their experiences then I would be happy to introduce you", or "My firm put together a guide to the rules and regulations affecting international business in [country]. Would you like a copy?"

Of course, this is just a simplified version of a conversation, but the formula is this:

Ask a good question.

Ask a follow up question.

Find things in common, ways that you could help.

Listening and following up

Bear in mind that you don't have to be so well prepared that you can always offer help "on the spot". It's just as effective to think about the conversation that you had with someone and then, a few days later, to email them to refer to some article that they might find of value, or to pass on some report or information that you have.

Peter works in an advertising agency and is a big sender of books. He reads many business books and if one relates to something that he talked about with someone he met then he buys a copy, writes a brief note inside it, and then posts it to the person he met. This just costs very little if you think about it in terms of advancing your career, yet it has a really big impact. So, if you find a book that you really enjoy, you can look out for opportunities to raise this in conversation with others, and if they are also interested you can use this as an opportunity to email them the details or to actually send them a copy of the book – in other words you can be proactive in planning this and raising related topics when you are networking face to face.

So he asks what he calls "leading questions". For example, let's say that Peter has just read a great book about how to manage international projects across many countries and cope with the fact that different nationalities approach projects in very different, and often frustrating, ways. Peter was interested to find that behaviour that may be absolutely normal in one country may come across as very rude or very inappropriate in another culture. So Peter can raise this topic of managing international teams and if the person he is talking to expresses an interest, he says that he will send details of the book (which in any case is a good way to have them offer up their contact details). But he doesn't send them the details, he buys an extra copy of the book, writes a message in it and sends it to them. Apart from the great impact this makes, it leaves the other person with something tangible that will remind them of the person who gave it to them.

Let's look at some generic questions that you can ask new people that you meet. Bear in mind that the more *tailored* the question is to that particular person, the better it is. So, a generic question might be "so what's happening internationally for you?" but a tailored one would be "I saw that you announced last week that you are ending manufacture in Germany and moving it to the Philippines. What does that mean for the future of your brand?" Once again this is where focus and passion are so crucial. Once you have chosen Geothermal Energy as your focus, you will start to know about the players in the industry and start to have the type of detailed knowledge that allows you to ask really good questions. However, you don't always need (or have the opportunity) to pre-plan questions – some great "starter" questions are set out below.

Examples of good questions

Who are your main competitors? How do you beat them?

Where are you seeing the best growth for your company?

How did you come to work for [your company]? Where were you before this? What's the biggest difference you saw between your two jobs?

What types of issues do you have to deal with – what lands on your desk? Who's in your team – how is your work type structured?

Where are you based? Do you have to travel a lot for the company?

Did you always plan to have this as a career?

What is the training like at your company? How do they support / invest in you?

Where do you see yourself in five years' time? What are your passions outside of work? Do you spend much time with your family? What do you enjoy most when you have time off?

What brought you to this event? What did you think of the last session?

What does [the trend for healthy eating] mean for your company?

How do you deal with international teams – what challenges does that create for you?

How do you find operating in [X] market?

How has the recent legislation change/entry of competitor affected your business?

What has been the biggest shift in your industry in the last few years?

Generic questions

These types of questions are fine for a first meeting, but because you just met this person, they are pretty generic. Once you have met someone and decided that they are relevant to you, then you need to start reading up on them, their company and their sector. One easy way of kicking this off is using Google Alerts and the other techniques set out in Chapter 3. By the next time that you talk to, or email, this person you should be talking much more specifically. For example, you should be saying things like "You mentioned when we met that your company was looking at setting up a new factory in Kazakhstan. I just came across this article that might be of interest to you".

Avoiding an interrogation

Armed with this knowledge that your role in the conversation is simply to have the other person talk about themselves, there is a risk that your conversation turns into something of an interrogation, with question following question. When someone is being invited to talk about themselves and their career that is not a massive problem, but it can start to feel a bit artificial. There are three techniques that are useful here:

- You should listen to the answer and delve deeper. In practice, once people move into questioning mode, they tend not to listen to the answer, but to start formulating the next question while the other person is talking. As a result, they don't pay attention to the answer. That's a mistake. It is better to listen and ask a supplementary question. For example, question: "What lands on your desk?" Answer: "Most of my time is spent on regulatory issues at the moment." Next question: "Tell me more about that. What types of regulatory issues does your company face?"

• You need to empathise and reflect back from time to time. That again is why having a focus or passion is so important because you will build up knowledge around a topic that will enable you to have views and opinions of your own. So, you might add, in the previous conversation "I have chosen Geothermal Energy as my main area of interest and I have heard a lot of people talking about the regulatory issues. What are the specific ones that hit you most?" Or, "That's interesting. I thought that the major issues were over funding as I have heard a lot of people talk about how the current oil price affects how much funding is available. What type of regulatory issues do you have to deal with?"

The crucial subtext here is – *I am interested in this topic as much as you and I have absorbed myself in it – I want to learn more from you.* By reflecting back every so often, showing that you have some knowledge and interest, this really encourages the other person to keep talking.

• What if you feel like you are running out of questions? If you are not sure what to ask next then it might be the time to say "Thanks, it's been really interesting talking to you, is it OK if I stay in touch?" or some similar exit line. However, if you want to keep the conversation going, there is a trick that you can use of just repeating back the last few words that the person said, but turn it into a question. It sounds a bit weird but it really works. It's apparently much used by Royalty who have to feign interest in a huge range of subjects in which they are going to have no interest or knowledge. Let's take the example of a minor Royal who has been asked to open a new sewage works. They turn up and are being walked around the facility by the proud manager. They come across a huge steel pipe and so the Royal might ask "Tell me what's going on here?" Our proud manger explains "The sewage is brought into the plant through this pipe." To which the Royal replies *"Through this pipe?"* To which the manager then carries on with an explanation of where it goes from that pipe and ends up saying "…….. and that then leads to the electric generators on the floor above." The Royal continues *"The electric generators on the floor above?"* and so on, for the next hour. This sounds quite strange, but it is well worth trying because you are going to be surprised at how well it works. It is a bit superficial but it achieves the main aim of having the other person talk.

The company, the role, the person

Remember also that there is a useful hierarchy of topics when you start to talk to someone new. Ask first about their company – this is very safe territory. The next layer is to talk about their role in the company – what are their main responsibilities, what do they particularly enjoy about their work, do they travel a lot and so on. That is more personal than just talking about the company but would generally not be seen as in any way intrusive. The third stage is to talk about them as an individual – that could be in career terms or about their life outside work. What do they do on holiday, what leisure pursuits or hobbies they have, what countries they like, their family and their career aspirations? You may not cover much in this third area at the first meeting or two, but there is real merit in making sure that you do start to explore these areas even if that doesn't seem entirely natural to you. The reason is that, while you can create some great networking around a person's career (which is what the first two areas do) it is rather impersonal and formal. Stronger and more personal relationships are formed where you have discussed and found empathies around the personal side as well.

This can be very natural for extroverts, but less so for introverts who don't feel so comfortable with this type of sharing. However, some element of personal empathy is really helpful in cementing relationships with new contacts if you can move onto it.

The real impact

What we have been doing here is being interested, not being interesting. Why does this matter so much. Firstly, it's because any attempt on your part to be interesting is pretty much doomed to failure – you are much more likely to come across as boring, self-centred or boastful in your attempts to impress.

Secondly, something very strange happens when you show an interest in another person and start them talking about themselves. This can best be illustrated by a wonderful story recounted on the radio by a former British Foreign Secretary. As a very senior member of our Government, he had to attend many formal dinners with visiting dignitaries and members of the diplomatic service. He was often expected to take his wife. One evening, after just such a formal dinner, our Foreign Secretary was in his official car, returning home with his wife. She complained that she had endured the most awful evening. What had happened? She explained that she had been seated next to the [name of country removed on legal advice] Ambassador, and as they sat down, she had turned to him and said "So, Mr Ambassador, you must have an interesting role. What are the issues that you are dealing with at the moment?" So a nice, polite way of opening a conversation. This had led to the said Ambassador talking non-stop about himself for almost five hours. Apparently, he had hardly drawn breath the whole evening. She had maintained something of a fixed smile throughout this tirade, occasionally saying "Really?" or "How interesting" but failing in any attempt to move the subject onto any other topic. Our Home Secretary apologised to his wife, promised to keep her closer to him at the next event and to think more about who was sitting next to her in future. He assumed that this would be the end of the matter.

However, he received a phone call the very next morning from the said Ambassador. It's worth repeating, word for word, what he said:

"I just wanted to tell you, that your wife is the most interesting person that I have ever met!"

This perfectly explains the strange effect it has on someone when you show interest in them – *they think that you are interesting.* You have to try this out – today – and see the impact. If you are doing it right then you will see how animated the other person becomes as they talk about themselves and their passions. And they will be left with a very positive impression of you.

There is a second leg to this building of strong and positive relationships – let's look at that now. Combining it with "being interested", this gives you **the secret of universal attraction.**

Empathy

What if you were told that you were going to meet someone and to sit next to them over dinner for several hours but that you have absolutely nothing in common with this person? Not only do you not have anything in common, but let's add that they like the opposite of everything that you like. Whether it is politics, leisure, the economy, religion or sport - anything that you can think about. How good a relationship do you think that you can build with this person? We think it's going to be a really tough evening. Here's why:

We are hard wired to *like people* who are *like us.*

The more that we have in common with someone, the easier it is to bond with them. So the trick is this – your job when you meet a *relevant person* is to find things in common. It doesn't matter what those things are:

You went to the same University

You both have three children

You both used to work at Deloitte

You live / used to live in the same County

You both know the same person / used to work with them

You take the same view on a recent news story

You travel to the same countries on business or for holidays

You are both enthusiastic skiers

There is a skill in this – which is that you need to range widely so that you can try to find things that you have in common. For example, you could ask geographical questions – "Have you always lived here in [London]?", "Do you travel with your work? What's the favourite City that you visit?", "I just returned from a great couple of weeks in Boston. Where do you like to travel to when you are on holiday?" – these tend to be safe "ins" to a conversation, and allow your target to either talk business or work as they wish.

Broaden the range

You need to range over family, education, holidays, how they won their job, where they grew up – as many points as possible and the more times that you can find a shared interest, connection, like or habit then the better. In reality, the more things you can find that you have in common with someone, the more empathy you are going to create. There is a bit of a game that you can play with this the next time you are with a group of people. Talk to each other in groups of two, for three minutes and see how many things you can find that you have in common.

A few words of warning on topics for discussion. It can be a great idea to avoid religion and politics because having contrary views to the other person can be fatal and can stop any relationship developing there and then. So try to avoid these topics in the early stages of any conversations. Once you know someone well, you may start to explore these topics but they are dangerous in the early stages. Somewhat surprisingly, we would also caution against talking about sport (particularly for men) and talking about family. This is based upon long experience.

For many, sport can be an apparently easy way to connect and create empathy – how often is an early question "what team do you support?" There are two issues around this. First, if you support opposing teams or are interested in completely different sports, this can be a dead end and sour the relationship early on. Secondly, a problem that we come across when coaching professionals on networking, is that you can easily become locked into a "sports buddy" relationship where all the conversations are about sport and nothing else. This can often mean that this is to the exclusion of any business relationship. Beware of this. Sport is definitely not a "no go" area and it can be a good way of breaking the ice, but beware of it interfering with building a business focussed relationship.

We have noticed that an equivalent topic is to talk about families, and while there can be great opportunities to build rapport and bond over similarly aged offspring or work/life balancing struggles, we have been told that, like sport talk, it can similarly be a hindrance. A very successful Senior Account Exec told of how she had built a fantastic relationship with one of her clients, they had great personal chats about family, but the conversations never turned around to the topic of business...for that, her client always engaged a colleague of hers.

The secret of universal attraction

However, *combine* – "being interested" with "empathy" and you have *the secret of universal attraction*. You can use this to connect with *anyone*. No matter how senior they are to you, no matter that you have never met them before, if you encourage them to talk about themselves and their interests and during that conversation you find a number of things you have in common then:

* They will instinctively like you

- They would describe you to others as an interesting person

- They will be keen to meet you and talk to you again

And if you think about that, it's a pretty amazing outcome from just an initial conversation. Keep in mind that the whole purpose of engaging with this person is so that you might find ways of helping them and it should enable you to remove any worries that you might have had from networking with people. It's worth thinking back to the list of worries that we made:-

- I might be left on my own with no one to talk to (while everyone else in the room is happily engaged in animated group conversations).

- If I start talking to someone then I don't know what to say to them.

- I might be stuck talking to somebody all night because I don't know how to end the conversation and move away.

- I'm worried that the conversation will just dry up.

- I don't know how to join a group of people.

- I forget people's names and then somebody else comes up and I cannot introduce them.

- I might end up talking to somebody very senior, and why would they want to talk to me. I will not know what to say to them.

- I am not sure what to do about business cards. Am I supposed to offer mine, or ask for one?

As you can see, we have covered every one of these. When you go into a networking event with the knowledge of how to deal with the physical side of networking and how to talk to people then there is no reason to be worried. Like every other skill it makes a huge difference if you practice it as you will grow in confidence the more that you do it. If you are at all nervous then you could try taking a friend with you to the first couple of networking events – provided you don't spend all night talking to that person!

Also bear in mind that a great way to start practising face to face networking is to do this at a social occasion, with friends or colleagues. It's low risk, you can have fun trying out the techniques that we discussed and it really doesn't matter if it's not absolutely perfect first time.

The most common reaction that we get from people that we teach to network is this. When they actually try it out, particularly the skill in having the other person talk about themselves, they can hardly believe how easy and effective it is!

What about me?

When we teach this "secret of universal attraction", people will often ask, "But when do I talk about myself?" That's a good question – in our experience you will find that as you engage with someone in this way they will ask you questions back. If so, but only if so, then you can respond quite naturally (without some need to boast or be massively impressive). This is where an "elevator pitch" can be useful – in other words if someone asked you to describe yourself (in a few words!) what do you say?

The clever bit here is to think in terms of what results you produce from your work or what special interests you have, rather than giving a generic answer like "I'm a lawyer" or "I am studying Economics at Exeter University". You are never going to lead with your elevator pitch, of course, because you are going to be *interested* in the other person so you are going to be asking them questions first. But you need to have an elevator pitch ready for if, or when, you are asked about yourself. You have the advantage that you can also link your own skills and interests back to the other person. Let's look at some examples:

"I'm passionate about the environment and I am studying law as it gives me a chance to make a difference. That was why I was particularly interested when you told me that your company had been working to reduce emissions from power stations."

"I've decided that I want to have a career in the music industry on the production side because I have been dabbling in computer generated music from an early age. I'm keen to meet people who have experience in music distribution which is why I came to this event."

"I have decided to specialise in team coaching at global companies. I have a background in languages and my company takes international teams and shows them how to work more efficiently with each other. That's why I was interested in how your company has coped with its new production facilities in Taiwan."

There is no need to agonise over the exact wording here – it's really about communicating your passions and areas of interest and flagging up what you are looking for and the type of people that you would like to meet or the type of activity that would help you.

This is really important – when you talk about yourself it should give the other person real guidance about what you are interested in, what your passions are, the type of future career that you are interested in.

This gives the other person a fighting chance of being able to help you – because if you are specific enough then they will most likely offer to introduce you to people that might be of help.

When running training sessions on face to face networking we are often asked "So if I am determined to be interested and have the other person talk about themselves, what happens if the other person has had the same training, so that they are determined that I will do most of the talking?" We have both experienced this and the good news is that it is fine! What happens is that there is a pretty equal amount of talking from both sides. It doesn't feel artificial or awkward – just that two people who are equally interested in each other have met.

SEVEN

DEVELOPING YOUR BRAND

When we talk to professionals about "brand" they can become quite defensive or dismissive, even confused "Why do we need to talk about brand? I'm not making shoes, I'm not a washing detergent". And it's understandable, brand has long been the sole realm of consumer goods, expensive cars and bags – so do we really need to develop a personal brand?

Pause that thought, and let's talk about reputation, both in a professional and personal context, ask yourself – what do people say about you? Then, even worse, what do they say about you when you're not in the room? What they say, is affected by your reputation, the traits and habits people project onto us from past experiences, interactions and their perceptions of the conscious and sub-conscious messages we give out. Your brand, is what people say about you when you're not there.

The exciting link to "brand" is this – like it or not, each one of us has a reputation and you have the choice to passively accept what is said about you, or take control of your own reputation, be pro-active and define your brand.

Then, ask yourself;

- What do people already say about me? What is my reputation? (Brand analysis)

- What would I like my personal brand to be? (Brand definition)

- What do I believe in? (Brand values)

- How will I make sure that people know about me – how will I raise my profile? (Brand awareness)

- How can I ensure that clients ask for me my name and come back again and again? (Brand loyalty)

Once you start to think in these terms, then the science of brand has some fantastic tools and methodologies that will make a real difference to how you are perceived, how differentiated you are and how valuable you are to other people! With these benefits, it's useful for the individual no matter what stage you are at in your career. At your very first interview, when you're trying to stand out from the crowd of other similarly qualified eager new graduates, a strong personal brand allows the interviewer an easier 'in' to you to assess whether you're a good fit for the work place, will help you to develop your personality and help you to build a personal connection with others. Similarly, when trying for a promotion or change of role, it allows others to easily imagine what your impact would be, because you have tangible and consistent associations with your personality, office behaviour and work. We all have favourite brands, brands we associate with and chose to purchase over others (no matter how rational we tell ourselves the purchase decision may be). By developing your brand, you are increasing the chances of the employer/client/colleague (even new partners and friends) liking what you have to offer.

But particularly, if you are at the start of your career you have a fantastic opportunity to decide exactly what type of brand you want to be – how you can develop and define yourself. If you are later on in your career, then you have the opportunity to refine your brand to make you more valuable or even to reposition yourself by using your knowledge of the market to find a unique gap or offer which you can deliver.

On a different, but related note, and linking to the rest of this book – when we network, we are striving to build connections, and many people struggle with what to say or how to conduct themselves in networking environments. Having a clearly defined brand for yourself allows you to streamline your communication and gives your new contact an easier grasp of who you are, and why they should be friends with you.

In other words, acting as professionals who are driven to deliver a really great service to clients we can learn from some of the most successful brands out there, they've defined who they are – and then consistently delivered it.

The foundation of brand

One of the best definitions of brand is that it is "a promise delivered". This encapsulates the principle that there is a clear offer and that it is consistently delivered. Lots of the largest brands were founded at a time when food was at great risk of being adulterated. By attaching a clear brand, the seller had an opportunity to build a reputation for quality, to differentiate his or her products from competitors and to create real value – even today the Kellogg's brand uses the line "If it doesn't say Kellogg's on the box, it isn't Kellogg's in the box" reminding consumers to "accept no imitations" (as best said by McCoys), because "it's always the real thing" (Coca-Cola).

There is a great risk that when we say brand, people think logos. A logo, is a way of flagging up what you're purchasing, the brand is much more than that, and it's where the real value can be found. The logo is there as a way of making it recognisable, a short cut that triggers a recollection of the underpinning brand values, the reputation of the brand and product.

As a professional person who is providing a service rather than a physical product, you have the ability to infinitely vary and adapt the service that you deliver. This gives you greater flexibility to adapt yourself to your clients needs far faster, but without a strong brand to provide consistency it can be confusing for the client.

To be successful, a brand has to be real. It has to address real needs in the marketplace, it has to be genuine (not just faking it) and it has to be delivered consistently, time after time. This last element is crucial. You cannot just create a brand in an instant. A brand (like a reputation) is built up over a period of time by consistent delivery.

Let's now start building your brand…

The four D's of brand success

To be successful, a brand must be desirable, differentiated and deliverable. Let's look at each of these in turn because they offer such valuable insights for a professional person who wants to build a successful career, particularly at a time of fierce competition.

The rules will apply whether you are just starting your career and looking for your first job (remember how Jess in Chapter 1 managed to create her environmental lawyer brand?). It can be just the same at the top of the profession where senior lawyers need to stand out and create real client loyalty. That enables them to build up a thriving practice and avoid just being played off against their competitors on price. After all, if a client can get pretty much the same service from another professional, then any sensible client would then start to choose on lowest price.

What is desirable?

It is quite natural for professionals to focus upon their own skills as the source of their reputation and value. For all professionals, high standards of qualifications and substantial on the job training is at the core of their being. Similarly, clients want their professional advisers to be well qualified and well trained. The problem with this "qualifications" approach however is that it is very 'common denominator' – you get to a certain level, and everybody has the same qualifications from comparably good universities. As we see post financial crisis, there are fewer jobs, and more people applying for them, competition in a semi-stagnant market is tight. The lesson from successful brands would be that you need to understand what it is that your clients really want and value, and position yourself accordingly. Take a look at bottled water, it's a commodity, water is water is water – and yet somehow, it's a booming multi-billion dollar industry with distinct brand personalities and benefits. Perrier has carved a niche out for itself as the artsy, quirky water, while Evian has positioned itself as fashionable, and filled with youthful vitality (remember, Evian Live Young?) with Smart

Water coming in as the new-kid telling everyone it really is the smarter water… even though they are all just H2O in a bottle. The trick that they all managed, was that they developed a strong brand that made them different (remember in earlier chapters when we talked about something that makes you stand out? Make it integral to your brand).

There is a startlingly easy way to find out what the market wants. That is to actually ask them. This would be a natural reaction if you were working as a professional in Marketing, Advertising or Brand, but may not be the first thought for an accountant, lawyer or actuary. Using the network that you are building up in Geothermal Energy (you hadn't forgotten, had you?) actually gives you an opportunity to talk to people who are in that industry, people that you would like to be working for, or working with as your future career.

The magic questions are these "What do great professionals do for you? What makes them better than the others?" and "What do the professionals that you use, sometimes get wrong, that can cause you problems?" It is important that these questions are asked in that order. Let's get positive thoughts first, and only after that can you look at shortcomings of fellow professionals. (Otherwise it just sounds like you are trying to dig out criticisms of others). You need to delve, ask deeper questions and really build up a picture of good and bad. You need to talk to as many people as you can so that you build up a balanced picture.

If looking for a job rather than a new client, the same questions can be tailored to talk about their 'pen portrait' of a 'model employee' – what are they looking for in a person? So a trainee accountant who has decided that she wants to work in the music industry will be networking with people in that industry and can say things like, "You must have had to deal with quite a few accountants in your time. Tell me, what did the best ones get right?" Or she may need to start by asking the people that she knows, "Who deals with accountants in your organisation? As I'm working on the finance side of the music industry, I think it would be really beneficial to gain a real understanding of how you use accountants, what works well and what doesn't work so well?" As a question, this fits well within the zone of asking people about themselves and works with the model of "being interested, not interesting".

Imagine after doing this that you are then at a job interview. Look at how differently you are going to present yourself! "I'm committed to working on the finance side of the music industry so over the summer I conducted interviews with [30] people working in that industry to try to understand what they wanted from their accountants, what they felt they were actually receiving at the moment and to identify any gaps that could be opportunities for me in my career". This is rather better than just turning up for an interview.

Understanding what is desirable to your target clients gives you the absolute foundation stone to start thinking about what type of an accountant, lawyer, management consultant or advertising expert you want to be. The closer that you can get to providing what your target market thinks is desirable, the more valuable you will be to them.

Differentiated

One of the hardest tasks for professionals today is to stand out, given that the general standard of professional service is typically very high and getting higher. You increase your value and your profile if you stand out from your competition (in a good way). The real starting point for this should be your research on what is desirable – after all, this is again what the great consumer brands of our time do, to avoid being driven into a price war.

In other words, if you are a lawyer, accountant, management consultant, actuary, whatever type of professional, it is an almost certain bet that your key competitors are just as good at being lawyers, accountants, management consultants or actuaries! If you look at your most similar competitors, could you honestly tell a prospective client that they couldn't do the work in question? Valuable differentiation, tends to be around enhancements (that are perhaps a little unexpected).

Differentiation occurs outside of the core service and is often about the way that you behave in delivering the service – it's the added electrolytes in water, the added benefit that makes it 'that little bit more special'. Let's look at each of those in turn.

Examples of an enhanced service would be:

- A client has a complex problem to solve with many different decision points. Rather than write a long letter of advice, the actuary prepares a single page flow chart so the client can see at a glance what different routes and outcomes are available.

- Beating deadlines. Agree with the client exactly when a particular piece of advice is needed and deliver it early!

- Being good at administration. Clients complain that their professional advisers are hopeless at billing on time, addressing the invoice to the right company and including all the necessary references. Ask your clients how they rate you on administration and then aim to become 100% compliant.

- Diarise key follow up dates for the client and show that you are thinking beyond the immediate issues by sending them diary reminders that they can accept and put into their diary.

Examples of delivering the service differently would be:

- Asking the client *how* they want the advice delivered. For example, one client was using the advice to complete a monthly Board Report, so the adviser used the Board template which meant that the client could cut and paste the advice, rather than rewrite it.

- A client was using the advice received to deal with an issue that was going to be raised at a quarterly Pension Trustees meeting. The meeting was due to finish at 4pm and the professional adviser rang the client at 4.30pm to check that everything had gone well at the meeting!

- Understand your client's passions and interests. Don't just see your role as delivering the contracted service, but as looking out for how you can help them in those passions. Make introductions to people that you know who share that passion, look out for events they could attend.

- Reframe your relationship with the client as, "my job is to make you more successful in your job." Talk to them about their aims, ambitions and challenges. Continually look for ways that you can help them. Make introductions for them, send them links to articles that may help them, invite them to relevant events.

It's about pre-empting the extra needs of your client and over-servicing them.

There is an exercise that we run when teaching groups of professionals which involves them listing all of the great experiences that they have received from other service providers. For example we may ask them to spend 15 minutes listing what was memorable and special about the service that they received at a hotel, restaurant, airline, shop or when buying online. Everyone has some good experiences to recount. The restaurant that always greets them by name, the hotel that keeps giving them the same room and the online store that replaced an item for free that was well out of warranty. David Maister, the author of "The Trusted Advisor" tells the story of having root canal work at his dentist and sitting down at 6:30pm that evening with his wife talking about the day when the phone rang and it was his dentist calling to check that David was okay and not in too much pain!

Once you have created that list of "memorably great service" then you can start thinking, "How am I going to stand out like that in the service that I provide as a professional?" That type of personal, caring, expanded service would make a great personal brand wouldn't it?

Deliverable

Everyone wants twice the service, for half the price. Very occasionally some disruptive innovation arrives which achieves that and changes the competitive landscape. But that is rare. So, in creating brand you, in creating the promise that you are going to deliver upon, you need to make certain that this promise is capable of being kept.

So unless you have discovered some service secret or new technology for delivery, promising to give twice the service of competitors, or promising to charge less than them for the same service, is going to be a short term success and a medium term disaster. You can win clients with those promises, but you will find it difficult keep them. In fact all the evidence is that it is better to under promise and over deliver, rather than the other way around (even though that is more typical). Think of a time you have been promised everything, whether it's a service or a product you've bought, only to realise you've fallen for a sales gimmick – do you want those emotions, the feelings of distrust and resentment to be associated with your brand?

To create positive association with your brand, think of clear ways to go above expectations. If we think of Avis, whose tag line was "we try harder", what would they do if they were an actuary or lawyer? Or, you could make a point of being "the professional who improves" and call the client, or even better visit them, after you have delivered a piece of work and ask how you could have improved it, so that you can learn for the next time.

It's not about delivering some perfect service at the lowest price. That is very unlikely to be sustainable. It is about being "just that bit different" from your competition. If you are not sure how to achieve that, then wait for the coming section on developing your brand.

One of the most important things to consider when developing your delivery promise, is that clients need to know what to expect. Those who have perfected their brand delivery get repeat work from the clients, because it is consistent every time. Clients will be quick to complain if the service drops below expectations and any good brand will be fast to respond, apologise and put things right. That's the real power of brands and why people are prepared to pay more for them. This is the prize that is on offer for professionals who develop a real personal brand. It creates client loyalty that is much less price sensitive.

No matter how wonderful the service is, that you have designed and delivered, it takes *time* to convert this into a brand. That's okay, because it also gives you an advantage over your competition. Just copying what you are doing does not mean they have achieved the same as you. The longer that you have been delivering your brand promise, the more it becomes associated with you and the more valuable it becomes. Copycats are seen as such and never achieve the same value in the mind of the client.

There is another way that you can think about personal brand – it's a technique that is both interesting and fun. It also helps you to think about how you are going to be distinctive, to stand out, and to *control* the effect that you are going to have on your clients and employers.

The joy of brands – three little words

One of the techniques that brand strategists use when desperately trying to find a way to distinguish one pot of identical yoghurt to the other 199 pots of identical yoghurt on the supermarket shelf is this. They ask the consumer what words come to mind when they think about a specific brand, or when they see its logo? Have a go now, what logos spring straight to mind – and what do they make you think and feel?

So, now that you have started to think in terms of being different and better than your competitors you can start to think about how you would encapsulate this *new you* into a personal brand, using commercial brand techniques. Use this thought, "A personal brand is the words that people would use to describe you, after you have left the room".

A great way of doing this is to ask the question the following, "If the person that I just met was asked to describe me in three words, what words would they use?" (just like for the identical yoghurt).

More to the point what words do you want them to use? So here's how you can run this brand building exercise to help guide you:

- Step 1. Email some clients and connections and ask them this question. Explain that you are carrying out a research project so that you can better understand client needs.

    "Can you give me the words that spring to mind when you think about the ideal [legal] [accounting] [management consultant] [etc.] adviser? I'm looking for words that describe the person rather than the firm as a whole."

    Send out as many of these email requests as you can because you are trying to get a good cross section of clients. If there are too few of them, then there is a risk of being skewed by a particular experience that one or two clients have had.

    Note: okay, so what if you're at the beginning of your career and you don't yet have a client roster you can utilise? If still at university, get involved in your university magazine and conduct a research piece for them on "the top things law firms look for in grad students", giving you an excuse to get in touch with industry professionals (remember – flattery, you're appealing to their superior knowledge…and ego). Alternatively, if you're junior in a company, make the most of 'water cooler moments' or be bold and reach out to the HR department.

- Step 2. Gather the data together so that you can see the most popular answers. You are looking to select 3 to 5 of these (before you end up with a final list of 3). This is your shortlist of words.

Note: are you seeing similarities, themes appearing and occurring? If so, great, you're already well on your way to delivering a consistent brand! If not, consider the following:

o *Pair the words up – are any of them related, conflicting, opposing? Where is this tension coming from?*

o *Dig deeper, and go back to people and ask if they'd agree with some of the other words you've been given in your feedback.*

o *Cast your net wider, and ask a broader range of people – do you then get any similarities or consistency, or is it similarly fragmented?*

• Step 3. Reach back out to your closest contacts, thank them for their earlier input so far, give them the shortlist of words and ask them "Next to each of my shortlisted words, what are the sorts of actions you think demonstrate this?" So, for example, a shortlisted word might be "Expert" and the behaviours might be "Writes articles", "Advises me of changes that are coming up in the future, not just the position now", "Is able to explain difficult concepts in plain English."

What we are looking for here, is to discover what behaviours you need to deliver. Your shortlisted words are going to be the words that your client thinks about after they have dealt with you. This is where your words need to be carefully chosen, it's great be dedicated – but does that mean clients expect you to be available 24 hours a day?

• Step 4. Have your final review and now list your three words. That's the personal brand that you are trying to create – as such, consider how they interact. Are there any contradictions amongst them? You don't just want to start delivering this brand, but you want also to make this an explicit part of your promise when you interact with people. Of course you may not always achieve perfect delivery, but you have set yourself a standard. Depending on your relationship with a client, you can always say something like "I always strive to be Responsive, Reliable and Consistent. How am I doing?" as part of your "sell".

And in case you are interested Alexis' three words are:

Helpful, international, irreverent.

While Kevin is aiming for:

Happy, helpful, h'expert

So, how do we evidence these? How do we bring our brand to life through our behaviours?

For Alexis, no matter what stage of the day or what else may be going on, if someone is in need (no matter how trivial it may be) he will not just offer help but will get stuck in and be there alongside that person. A firm believer in team work and everyone crossing the finish line together, he has to live being *help-ful* through his actions. Having lived *internationally*, and travelled extensively for work and pleasure, asking himself, and clients, "So how does this connect to what we're seeing in other places?" or "What can we learn from X market that dealt with similar issues?" is the norm. It's about expanding the lens through which we look at challenges to encompass more than the original location or market…it also means being the one who jumps on the plane to get face to face for conversations rather than dialling in from separate countries. Some may baulk at the use of *irreverent*, thinking that it can be negative and disrespectful or not taking things seriously, but used from a positive position it breaks Alexis free from assumptions – why do we always have to do it the same way? Challenging assumptions, because you're not ham-stringed by a sense of "this is how it <u>has</u> to be done because that's just how it's done" leads perfectly into Alexis' career in innovation. As John F. Kennedy said "don't ask why, ask why not?" – irreverence at its best!

For Kevin *happy* means, for example, that when entering a meeting, going into the office building, when seeing a client or someone new, he will make certain that he is smiling broadly. Even if it's the end of a tough day or he is jetlagged after a long flight. Personal brand is about exhibiting the right behaviours even when there's some real effort involved. Similarly, being *helpful* means giving up personal time for others – and time is always valuable. It may mean putting his own priorities on hold. Being *expert* means that Kevin wants to be sure that he has read everything relevant and spoken to many friends and colleagues with expertise before trying to teach or pass on knowledge to others. In his declared areas of Pricing and of Business Development, it is this expertise that people are paying money to use. It is the acid test of his real value to clients.

Delivering your promise

There is a price to be paid by you in return for creating a strong personal brand. The price is that you need to be really committed to delivering on your personal brand. Being "helpful" means putting yourself out, going the extra mile, really giving to others. There will be times when you are tired, or times when it would just be a lot easier not to offer any help. However, our experience has been that the price you pay in terms of giving delivery of your service consistent with your chosen personal brand will be repaid many times over in terms of reputation, value and rewards. Or would you accept being "just the same as all the others"?

EIGHT

THE SCIENCE OF ATTRACTION

What makes you like someone? What are the factors that will decide that you like Julia, but that you don't like Will? Researchers have realised that this is a fascinating subject for every human being, particularly as most but, surprisingly, not all, people do exhibit a reasonably strong desire to be "liked". In fact there is a good evolutionary reason for this. You can increase your chances of survival and of flourishing if you have the support of others rather than their indifference or their enmity.

So, on the assumption that you are neither a dictator or gang leader (where the use of force to obtain assistance, as opposed to using liking, is a viable alternative) then understanding how you might be liked is actually valuable knowledge for you. A useful foundation for this is to understand that it is *not* about turning yourself into some false, artificially created "likeable person". We may have come across people like that and primates seem to have an instinctual ability to detect that type of falsehood.

So, just as with so many of our networking skills, the key to being liked is to look at and understand the other person, rather than focussing on yourself. There are essentially three dimensions to liking that we are going to use in networking.

Similarities

We mentioned in the previous Chapter the importance of finding things that you have in common with people that you meet, because *we like people who are like us*. Interestingly, this effect is contextual, it changes depending upon the surrounding circumstances and in particular by the rarity of the similarity. Let's look at an example.

Gareth is an Account Manager at a famous brand agency. He is on holiday with his wife Kath in Laguna Beach, just midway between Los Angeles and San Diego. It's the last day of what has been a wonderful holiday with their six year old daughter, which included a magical visit to Disneyland and then a whole week on the beach in an artists' colony and beach resort. Gareth and Kath have wondered many times whether they should move the family to America. They visited regularly and had always enjoyed meeting American people and they just worried if they were seeing a "holiday effect" when it might be quite different to live and work in the US.

That last evening of the holiday they were at a restaurant across the road from their hotel, reflecting on the stunning beauty of the Californian coast and once again wondering if they should move countries, or at the least investigate this further. As they are talking about this they hear the sound of very British voices from a table close to them where a couple happen to be talking about life "back home". This is such a coincidence, as you don't find that many Brits in Laguna Beach and they are talking about life back in Britain, just as Gareth and Kath are thinking of leaving it. Gareth calls over to the couple and says "Hello, it's nice to hear voices from back home". That's enough for them all to get a table together, during which Gareth and Kath find that their new friends are Brits who relocated to live in California two years ago, so how useful is that! Here is the perfect and fortunate chance to find out what it's like to relocate. What are the good things and the bad things about working in this part of California?

Here's what's interesting. Had it not been in a foreign country, Gareth and Kath would certainly not have approached a couple at another table. It was having something unusual in common that made this possible, both being Brits in an area where that was unusual and then both talking about the contrast between the UK and the US at the same time.

So, the more unusual the similarity that you find, the more connected each of you will feel. A great way of delivering on this is to either range widely in your conversations so that you might uncover strange things that you have in common, or look for that online after you have met a relevant person for the first time, for example by having a good look through their LinkedIn Profile.

Don't worry if you draw a lot of blanks as you range across various topics. You can find that you were born on different continents, that you support entirely different sports, went through radically different educations and experiences. However, then you find that you both had a Labrador as a pet when you were growing up, or both collected Pokemon Cards and you are off on building a warm relationship. Just focus on the things that you *do* have in common.

To this end, while we advise asking questions and strongly focusing on them rather than you (as mentioned in earlier chapters) if conversation isn't taking off (some people just aren't great at talking about themselves) you may wish to try dropping "hooks" for them to pick up on. These are small nuggets of information that tease at a bigger story from your end, which allows them an easy topic to latch onto and reassures them that it's okay to talk.

Compliments. *You are so clever – and strong*

Compliments are such an easy and effective way of making someone like you, that it is a real surprise that they are so little used. A well-aimed compliment will be remembered warmly by the recipient for a very, very long time. If you think back to the last time you were complimented you will find that it reawakens all of the warm feelings that you had when you first received it.

Now it is obvious that false compliments are a real turn off. Someone who throws compliments around too freely will come across as false and smarmy. That is really easy to avoid in practice.

For a compliment to work it simply needs to be grounded in a reality about that person, and you simply need to flag up what it is that you like about them or their company. So, for example, if you know anything positive about the company that the person works for, then you should be quick to mention it. You are going to be surprised by how positively most people view the company that employs them. Of course there can be exceptions, but the general rule is to be strongly supportive. So you might point out that their company is the largest, or most famous or fastest growing or whatever. If you have had good personal experience of using their company then you should say so. On this point, a business friend of ours, General Counsel for a large telecommunications provider is shocked by the number of people he will meet at events who tell him, sometimes in great detail, about their struggles and issues with the company he works for and the service they have (or haven't) been provided with. Overwhelmingly people are loyal to their employers, so if you do get chatting to an employee of a company you have a long-standing gripe with – don't go there. As your mother once told you, if you can't say anything nice, don't say anything at all.

Once you have them talking about their own role you can look for the positives in what they are doing. So you might say "that sounds like a lot of responsibility" or "tell me more about the strategic changes you are making – they sound pretty cutting edge". When they talk about how they came to join their present company or why they left the old one you might say, "It sounds like you made the right move".

If they start talking about their competitors and how they are coping in the market you might say "That sounds like a great initiative, tell me more about what that means in practice."

You can see it is just being positive about what they and their company are doing. If you are meeting with *relevant people* then you already have shared passions with them so this should be easy. After all they are living out a career that really interests you. So it's just a matter of finding ways to be positive about their career choices and what they are achieving.

This really comes down to this practice – "catch them doing something right, and then tell them so". Not hard to do and devastatingly effective in helping someone to really like you.

One of the things people like being told is that they were right, that they spotted something interesting that you hadn't thought about or that you agree on some topic. So while you are making a point you can use phrases like this:

- It's just like you were saying. The fastest way to create a team feeling is to have a social event.

- I hadn't thought about that, but you are right. What we need to do is to focus on clarifying the strategy, before we start worrying about the tactics.

- I feel exactly the same way. I worry that although my boss spent considerable time training me when I started work, I am probably not spending as much time as I should be on training those who work for me.

All of these reinforce the great warm feeling that they are having from engaging in a conversation with you. That you are like them, that you have common feelings but they are delivering some useful insights that you would not have thought of on your own.

Kevin has lunch regularly with a very charismatic friend – someone who reached the heights of leading Business Development at a Big Four accounting firm.

About half way through each lunch Mr Charisma will say something like – "That's what I like about you, you are very good at spotting the key issues" – or, "Well you are good at that – you always give really practical advice". He gives these brilliant compliments while looking directly into your eyes and smiling. It feels great to be on the other end of compliments like these. Don't fake it, but when the other person does something that you like or says something that is clever, pause and tell them. This is really transformational. Try it today!

Co-operation

The third dimension to "liking" is around alignment of interests – in other words are you and the *relevant person* headed in the same direction and are you supportive of them. Here again is where focus becomes so crucial – if you are following your personal interests and passions then that enthusiasm will shine through.

How do you then show that you have objectives that are aligned with theirs? By using the questioning techniques that we have set out in this book and have the other person talk about:

- Their company

- Their own role in company

- Their personal agenda, both inside and outside of work

The more that you encourage them to talk by questioning, listening and delving deeper ("that's really interesting, tell me more about how you did that") then the more opportunities you will find to think of ways that you might be able to empathise ("I feel the same way", "I found the same thing", "I like that too", "I went there on holiday as well") or to find ways to offer help. Help could be introductions to people, sending book and articles, links to relevant YouTube or TED.com videos – anything really that shows your shared interest.

And if you find that you don't have things in common or have opposing views on issues. Well you can just move on. There will be many other people to meet who are going to share your views so we absolutely advise against "faking it" and pretending to have things in common or shared interests that you don't have. That's wearing for you and unlikely to be convincing to the other person. Be really polite but move on and find other people.

The power of storytelling

Another area of research has been the impact of storytelling and the effect that it has on your listeners. Of course whole cultures and religions may have a rich culture which derived from the telling of stories from one generation to another. It may be the glue that binds a culture together, giving a shared sense of history.

There is a brief summary of this in the expression "facts tell, stories sell". Stories have an ability to tap into the emotional side of people and can be really powerful in creating a sense of shared purpose and background. We like people who are like us.

We are not thinking of fictional stories here, but of how you bring out your experiences in terms of storytelling rather than reciting facts. Stories are powerful and memorable. Take the example of a group of Venture Capitalists who run regular "Dragon's Den" sessions for budding entrepreneurs to pitch to them for funds. There are six or so presentations a day of pretty variable quality and it can be both tiring and quite boring for the Venture Capitalists sitting through this.

One afternoon, they see a man in his early 30s who is looking for funding for a biotech company that he founded after he graduated from Medical School. He started his presentation like this. "When I was 8 years old, my Dad was walking me to school at our home town in Concorde, Massachusetts. He travelled a lot so when he did get time at home he was really involved with me and my younger sister. He read us bedtime stories, took us to school and would be there waiting for us at the end of each day. It was a crisp November morning and I can remember that the sun was shining and the leaves were that beautiful red, brown, bronze colour and were piled up against the perimeter fence of my school. As we reached the school gate my Dad suddenly grasped at his chest. He was having a massive heart attack. He dropped to the ground and died in front of me. I decided that day that I would devote my life to medical research so that no other 8 year old boy would go through that experience."

Do you think he got his funding?

Now, you probably cannot beat that, but you can think of illustrating your experiences with stories rather than facts. This can also be explained in how you describe yourself. "I have a great sense of humour." (That's a tell). Or, "I am an expert. I know this because no less a man than the Nobel Laureate, Nils Bohr, described an expert as "Someone who has made every possible mistake in a very narrow field of endeavour", and that's definitely me!" (That's a sell). Let's look at a real example:

"I have always been interested in healthy eating, not in an "eat it because it's good for you sense" but because I was brought up for three years when I was a child in a jungle village on a small island in Malaysia and fantastic, fresh, wonderful food was all around me. Only when I returned to "civilisation" did I realise how much I missed that. So I became interested in how we can all have an enjoyable and really healthy diet without having to move back to the jungle!"

Make it personal

In personal and in business relationships, people can be surprisingly lazy when it comes to making friends with or impressing others. How often do we send a box of chocolates or some flowers, how often are there generic invites to sporting events or to pretty boring seminars?

A gift, no matter how small, makes much more impact if it relates specifically to something the other person said to you, because it shows that you were listening

(!) and that you were interested in and attentive to what they said. Some real life examples:-

- You said that you had to manage international, cross cultural, teams and so I thought that you would find this book ("When Cultures Collide") really interesting.

- You mentioned that you had a labradoodle puppy and I thought that you might find this website interesting as it gives a lot about the history of the breed.

- You said that you were going to Zermatt for the first time for a skiing holiday next month so I had my friend who is a regular there put together some recommended runs and a guide to the best bars and restaurants.

    Remember – it's all about them!

NINE

ONLINE NETWORKING

Your online presence is now an absolutely crucial part of who you are and how you present yourself to the world. It cannot be ignored – even if you are not a great fan of online activities. Others will judge you by what they find out about you online. If you have not paid real attention to this then it will seriously count against you. In addition, learning how to be proactive online is a fantastic way of creating and maintaining networks and can put you ahead of the competition – without ever leaving your desk or making small talk over canapés.

There are two primary routes to online success – LinkedIn.com and Twitter - so we will look at each of these individually.

LinkedIn.com

With more than 200 million members and 2 more joining each second, this is the number one networking tool in the world. Although it started in the USA, it has great coverage now in Europe and Asia. If you have not yet set up a (free) profile on LinkedIn then instructions on how to do this and how to add the LinkedIn logo to your email signature (so that recipients can just click on the logo to be taken to your public profile) are set out in Appendix I to this book. So from here on in, we are going to assume that you have set up your profile, uploaded a photo and started adding Connections.

We *cannot overestimate* the importance of LinkedIn to business networking. It enables you to gain work, job offers, new connections, to raise your profile – and you can achieve a lot of this while sat at your desk or on your mobile phone or tablet. You can use it as a "filler" when you have a few minutes spare. We typically look at LinkedIn at least 3 or 4 times a day! Many people are quite passive about LinkedIn and this is a big mistake. Sitting there with an unimpressive profile description and a few hundred connections is not rewarding. However, if you know how to use LinkedIn properly, you will be amazed at just how powerful it is.

Your Profile

Not only the first thing that people see when they look you up on LinkedIn (as they will, once they have met you) this is likely to be one of the top results they will see if they just search on your name in Google, Bing or any search engine. This is one of life's rare opportunities to write your own script and choose what people read about you. Given how important it is, it really does deserve some proper time and attention to get right, and needs to be reviewed *at least* every 6 months to be updated and refined.

It should be written in the first person – "I am particularly interested in Geothermal Energy and its application to energy conservation in cities." Strangely, some people put this in the third person even though they wrote it themselves, which is just plain odd "Graham is a results focused Team Leader who thrives on challenging situations". You profile is a golden opportunity to spell out your area(s) of focus and to say exactly what you are looking for. Examples would be:

> "I have a real interest in Geothermal Energy and in particular the use of heat pumps to save money (and save the world) at the design stage of office and industrial buildings. I am planning to build my career in this area and am interested in hearing from others with the same interests.

I am also studying for a Masters in Management and have enjoyed the use of statistical analysis in strategy formulation. If you work in this area then get in touch as I would like to understand what career opportunities exist?"

This splits into two different interests so that it opens up two possible career routes. To find other ideas have a good wander around LinkedIn and look at other peoples' profiles, particularly those who share your interests. Provided that you break it up with paragraphs, there is no reason to keep the information in your profile short, you have up to 2000 characters and that gives plenty of scope. If you have particular achievements to list then that's fine too – but don't worry if it is early on in your career as it is just as valuable to describe your interests in plenty of detail.

Let your enthusiasm show through – that's important. Do not be too serious and factual. One good profile that we saw started off "I have always been a foodie and from early on I wanted that to be my career as well."

Fill in as much as possible of the background information and skills that are available within LinkedIn. The general rule is that the more detail the better because, when others are looking at your profile, they will be looking for things that they have in common with you (this is important in creating empathy between you both). So holiday jobs, travel and other after work interests are important too.

If you have something particularly unusual that you did, like looking after Colin the lemur at a zoo during your summer holidays as a temporary job, then put that in as well. Think about something that people will remember about you, it doesn't have to be relevant to your career. A good friend started his career as a sound engineer at the BBC. From time to time he would work with world famous artists and whenever he did, he would wear a pair of white cotton gloves. Time after time, he found that great artists on their return to the UK would ask to work with "the sound guy with the white gloves". He knew that they were unlikely to remember his name, but they would remember the gloves. It lead to him knowing and becoming good friends with some really interesting people.

The detail and effort that you put into your profile is absolutely *crucial* to future success. It is not at all unusual to receive job interviews through recruitment agencies and head-hunters just based upon the details in your profile and you can expect anyone who is thinking of making contact with you to check out your Profile online. It has become the *new first impression* and we all know how important that is. Spend several hours making it right, send it to friends and ask for their views. Have a good look at people that you connect to on LinkedIn, especially those that share your passion, for ideas on how to use this space.

In addition, the more detail and information that you put into your profile, the more chance that someone reading it will have something in common with you. We have looked at the importance of empathy and that "we like people who are like us", which means people with whom we have something in common. The more facts and information that you include about yourself, the more chance there is that there will be something in common with the reader. This is an important cornerstone of strong relationships.

Make sure that you include a suitable photograph of yourself in the Profile. It should be fairly (or very) formal although you can match your career type, so someone heading for the advertising industry could be more casually dressed than someone who aspires to be a lawyer. Again this is a key "first impression" point for you. You will be judged based upon what your picture says about you. Make sure that you are smiling in your photo!

Finally, you can now add slideshows of presentations you made and even video to the end of your profile, if you have this type of material that you can usefully share.

In the privacy and settings area of LinkedIn (found by hovering your mouse over the thumbnail of you at the top of the page) you will find an on / off switch for activity broadcasts. If you are working on your Profile or improving your photo you should *first* switch this to off, then make your changes, then switch it back on. Otherwise all your connections will be notified that there are changes, when it may just be you doing some spring cleaning of your profile.

Adding Connections

LinkedIn is a numbers game. Provided that they are actually "connections", then the more people you can connect to, the better. So what is a connection? It means somebody that you actually "know". What does that mean? When teaching this, we found an interesting difference between "horizontal relationships" (with people at a similar level to you) and "vertical" relationships (with people more senior than you). With horizontal relationships you can be quick to connect. You will find that others are quick to accept and this helps to build up the number of connections you have that could be useful to you in your future. For vertical relationships it's generally best to connect only once you "know them" so they don't feel that you are moving too fast. There is a real element of judgment here. If you met someone at an event but spent quite a lot of time talking with them (not at them!) then you may both feel comfortable connecting after that. For other people it may come after several meetings or conversations. The reason for not connecting vertically too quickly is this – you really need to be able to contact this person on behalf of one of your other connections and be able fix up a meeting. Do you know them well enough to do that? You can see that this means that if you only met someone senior (a vertical) very briefly then you should not connect to them. However, if it was one of your "friends" (a horizontal) you might be fine with making the introduction.

"Internal" connections are just as valuable as external ones because raising your own profile within your organisation (University or workplace) is valuable to you, and you don't know with whom these internal connections are themselves connected. We are often asked, "Should I connect with all of my University friends or all of the people that I work with?" The answer is a definite yes, so long as you actually "know" them, as we have defined it.

Joining Groups

One of the great strengths of LinkedIn is "groups" where likeminded people meet together to share experiences, ask questions, ask for help with research and offer advice. It is important that you join relevant groups and that you join in the conversations as soon as you feel confident to do so. If you do join in, then it is acceptable to ask for advice or to share opinions or details of useful events, conferences or seminars that are coming up, but *do not* ask for a job! As explained in Chapter 4, First Impressions, the important thing is to give before you expect anything in return, although it is fine to ask for advice or to show interest in another person's area of expertise.

If you search LinkedIn (use the search box on the front page) you can then type in your area of interest, for example, "Geothermal" and you will find that there are groups, with several thousand members, dealing with this topic. Most groups are open, which means that you can join instantly. Some are locked and this just means that your application to join is sent to the person who set up the group for approval.

You should join as many groups as you can find that are relevant to your interests and passions because this can be a great way to raise your profile and to learn more about your topic. When you first join a group then it is good practice to look at the various discussions that are taking place. It's both a great guide to matters that are of current interest to group members and is a way of keeping up to date. Once you have a feel for the type of discussions that are taking place you can join in the conversations and add your own viewpoint. Or you can start a discussion. This doesn't need to be about you giving out some amazing insight. It is just as useful (for networking) if you ask a question or ask for help, for example, "I am writing an essay / article on the barriers to Geothermal Energy replacing wind power as a green energy source. Does anyone have views on the real world issues affecting this?" Or how about, "I am just starting out in my career and I'm really fascinated by Geothermal Energy. Can anyone suggest group events I can attend / the best sites for me to visit to keep up to date?"

Being active in groups, joining in or starting conversations, makes a huge difference. It raises your profile and lets you see who are the most active people in your area of interest. You can also message any other group member directly, for example to make a comment to them about something they wrote or to ask for some advice. Usually you need to be connected to someone to message them directly (or use your limited number of InMails) but you can freely contact other members of a group at the time of writing this book (although these were rumours this might stop).

Just like any other type of networking the core principle is to *try to help others*, but given the general friendliness within groups you could also ask for some help and advice on a problem that you are struggling with. Just make sure that you do not ask anyone for a job or for too much help. It's a judgement call, but people soon identify others who are "takers" rather than collaborators and helpers.

One thing that we have noticed inside groups is that if you have something to give away that is valuable to members you will often receive many requests for it. For example, if you have conducted a piece of research, gathered together data on a topic, conducted surveys etc. then you should flag that up in your newsfeed inside the relevant group and just add "contact me if you would like a copy." A great way of helping others and making new connections.

If you have a particular interest that is not well served already, then it's easy to start your own group. Just give it a name and invite people that you think would be interested, for example from your existing connections or people that you have come across in other groups. Remember that you can contact them just because you are in the same group.

Using Empathy

Need to contact someone? Now that you are active on LinkedIn then you should look at their Profile before you speak to, or email, them so that you can find out something that you have in common, and then refer to that.

Let's give you an actual example. Mariano is a partner in the biggest firms of Facilities Managers in Spain. He was meeting with a Director at an important client, who told Mariano that he needed to contact Angela, a colleague of the Director because "she is very senior and she is running the project that you are interested in". The Director made an email introduction for Mariano to Angela on the basis that Mariano would then phone her and arrange a meeting. When Mariano arrived back at his office his pulled up Angela's Profile on LinkedIn and saw that she had, many years ago, worked at a bank in Australia. Coincidentally, Mariano had met the Property Director of that Australian bank in Madrid about six months earlier.

So Mariano's conversation with Angela started by saying that he saw from her Profile that she used to work in the particular bank and asked if she knew the Director that he had met? It turned out that he was actually Angela's boss there. As a result Mariano and Angela spent some time talking about her experiences at the Australian bank and then Mariano fixed up to meet her for a coffee the next day at a café close to her offices. They met and Angela bought Mariano a coffee and a chocolate cake! They had established something in common through LinkedIn and that empathy had led to her treating Mariano like an old friend even though Mariano was the one who wanted to see her. And he wanted to see her, so that she could give Mariano some help on an important project.

Mariano and Angela had a much warmer first conversation and the meeting stated in such a friendly way solely because they had found something they had in common and talked about that first. Try this technique and you will be amazed at how effective it is. Mariano had no worry about talking to her about something that was on her LinkedIn profile. He wasn't worried that she would think he had been "checking up on her". People tell us that they are worried that if they talk about someone's LinkedIn profile it will surprise the other person. Bear in mind that you are only talking about information that this person themselves typed into their Profile and made public. It is what they want people to know about them. If anything it just comes across as more professional that you read about them before calling. This is a really important routine to build up. Before you talk to someone look them up on LinkedIn. We have even done this just minutes before meeting someone new to us by using the LinkedIn app on a smartphone.

Location Searching

Going somewhere? Whenever you are visiting another city it is worth thinking about whom you might like to meet while you are there. Select advanced search on the front page of LinkedIn and that brings up the opportunity to make a search by country / city / postal code. Just type in your destination and it will show existing Connections of yours who are close to that location. Here's what you will find:

- There may be 1st connections there. These are people you know directly, so this is a great opportunity to grab a coffee or something to eat and re-establish your contact. Just like any friendship, business friendships thrive on contact and wither away if left alone.

- You will also see "2nd connections". *These are really interesting* because it means that although you don't know them, someone who is a 1st connection to you does know them, and could make an introduction for you to meet them. This is a very useful flag. It is always worth looking through these "2nd connections" in case there is someone that you would like to meet. If you do, then just make contact with the 1st connection of yours who knows them, and ask for an introduction.

- You will see that there are various filters on the results page of the searches, so that you can narrow down the search and, for example, see people who are in the same LinkedIn groups as you. For these, as you are in the same group you can contact them directly through LinkedIn and as you have a shared interest there is no harm in suggesting a coffee.

There is also a mobile phone app called "Here on Biz" which gives out your location in your update feed when you visit a new city and can also show you which of your connections are currently nearby. You may need to use it with care as once you launch it, then it broadcasts your location, but it can be a great way to find useful people who would be happy to meet up with you. It can even show you relevant people who are on the same flight as you or staying at the same hotel if they are also using the app. Like all apps, you need to consider the privacy options around using this.

People you may know

On the right-hand side of the front page of LinkedIn you will see a column, which gives suggestions of people that you might know (for example based upon places where you were employed, connections that you have in common with other people or Groups). You will normally find two or three of these are shown on the front page and if you click the words "people you may know" it take you to a separate page which gives a continual list of suggestions. You just keep scrolling down.

You can find some fantastically valuable connections through this route. For example, a colleague tells the story of seeing a name suggested in this area of a lady who was a director of an important target client for him. He didn't know her, he certainly would like to know her. When he clicked on the "connections in common" he found that one of his old colleagues from a previous job was the link. First, he noticed that this old colleague had changed jobs and was also now working in a company that he would love to have as a client. So he now had a good reason to contact him, find out how things were going in his new job and suggest that they meet up for a coffee. Then, he asked his old colleague how well he knew the director that had been flagged up by LinkedIn. He was told that they were close friends having known each other for more than 10 years. So he followed this up by asking if his old colleague could arrange a coffee so he could meet this director. It's a great story. Just by looking at the entries in "people you may know" he re-established contact with an existing connection and obtained a warm introduction to a target director.

Looking at this list of "people you may know" is an important activity. If you see someone in this list that you don't know, but that you would like to know, then you will see that the connections that you have in common are listed. So think about asking one of these connections to make an introduction for you to the new person. This is one of the biggest benefits of using LinkedIn.

The newsfeed

When you log onto LinkedIn, the first thing you see is the newsfeed which gives new stories of relevance to you, updates from groups that you have joined, news from your connections and other information that has been entered into the "sharing box" that appears at the top of the page. Once again, here is a source of really valuable information. You will see news of people changing jobs which gives you an opportunity to congratulate them and then to contact them after a few months to see how their new role is working out. You will see news of events that you might want to attend and your connections may well be giving you valuable links and suggestions on areas on interest to you. After you have been on LinkedIn for a while and have joined the relevant groups and added the right connections, you will find that there is useful information in your newsfeed every single day. So much so, that the front page of LinkedIn has very much become our default site, by which we mean the site that we go to when we have a few minutes spare during the course of a day.

You can do this not just when sat at your desk but also on your smartphone or tablet. Quite often you are able to "like" a comment made by somebody else in your network or to comment with your own thoughts and again this is a great way of staying in contact with your connections and adding value to them. For example, Kevin recently posted a link to an article he found talking about the spread of virtual education (to degree level) because he knew that this is something that is of interest to many of his connections. One of these replied by directing Kevin to another site, which gave date details of a whole range of courses being conducted online, of which he had previously been unaware.

It means that you are continually being kept up-to-date on matters that are of real interest and value to you.

Tracks

If you look at someone's profile on LinkedIn while you are logged in, then it leaves a track showing that you looked at their Profile. So when they next log into LinkedIn they will see on the right hand side of the page a note "who's viewed your profile" and underneath that is a link. If they click on the link then they see a list of who has been looking at them. We have friends who are quite happy about this. If they are interested in someone, then why not "show them" that? In return for your leaving these tracks, you are also able to see who has been looking at you. On the front page when you log into LinkedIn, you will see on the right hand side a note, for example "your profile has been viewed by 3 people in the last 7 days". If you click on this, you will be taken to a list so that you can see who has been looking at your profile.

You can turn this feature off so that you do not leave tracks when you view someone else's profile. To do that you go to privacy and settings (found by clicking on the thumbnail picture of you at the top of the page) and once on the Privacy + Settings page you will see that you have a choice to limit the information that the other person can see when you have viewed their Profile. For example you can choose to hide your name in which case it would say "Someone in the [Finance Industry] based in [London] viewed your profile". This will not necessarily hide your details because if the other person clicks on that statement they will see a list of people who *could* match that description, so they might well see your details in that list. The other alternative is to switch off tracks altogether in which case the other person will see "An anonymous LinkedIn User viewed your profile". If you have a free account with LinkedIn then in return for being anonymous, you will also be unable to see who viewed your profile. This might encourage you to upgrade to a paid account on LinkedIn which allows you to switch off your tracks while still seeing who viewed your profile. Up to you.

We do regularly look at the list of who has viewed our profiles. Often it happens just before someone invites us to connect, or makes contact with us in another way. On other occasions it has reminded us of a person we had not made contact with in ages and stimulated us to make contact with them. Once, it was an old business contact who had moved from London to Washington. This actually stimulated an opportunity to connect with someone with whom we had lost contact and largely forgotten.

Email signatures

One you have a LinkedIn profile, you should be advertising that fact. One of the best ways of doing that is to add the freely available logo blocks as part of your signature at the end of emails. You can see an example of this on the next page:

The point is that anyone receiving an email from you has a short cut to seeing your LinkedIn profile by clicking on the LinkedIn logo. See Appendix II for details of how to set this up.

Status Updates

On the front page of LinkedIn you will find a blank box next to a picture of you, ready for you to type in a useful update. You can also link this to your Twitter account so that any updates here are repeated in your Twitter feed (but only the first 140 characters).

Well used, this is a brilliant way of raising your profile, contacting the right people or organising events and meetings. Let's look at some of the ways that you can use the status update:

- If you have seen an interesting article online then you can link others to it through the status update. Just type in "Great piece of research on how empathy is created" then hit return and then type in (or paste) the web address. LinkedIn automatically displays a thumbnail of the site so that you can see the page you are referring to. Status updates appear in the newsfeed of all of your connections on LinkedIn. They can then click on your wording or on the thumbnail to go directly to that site.

  If you are repeating your status updates in Twitter then bear in mind the need to stay within 140 characters (although LinkedIn will itself shorten the web address you use).

  We have friends who are wonderful at this – they use automated search tools (like Netvibes and Google Alerts) to scour the net for items using key words around their areas of interest, then post status updates referencing what they found at different times throughout the day. A fantastic way of raising your profile and delivering real value to your connections.

- Attending an event or visiting a new city – post an update so that your connections will know what you are up to and can meet up with you for a coffee if they are in the same area.

- Ask for help. Maybe you are carrying out research or stuck for an answer to a specific problem. You could send out a help request (although use sparingly because it could be seen by all your connections and may be irrelevant to many of them. It is probably better to use groups for these requests because this is more focussed).

- Tell people what you are up to? Probably not. That may be OK on Twitter, but unless you have some real value to give and (usually) a good link to pass on, then it is unlikely to look right on LinkedIn. We have seen this work for a well thought through opinion piece, where the poster put a link to their own blog on the status update, and that was both useful for readers and drew traffic into the writer's site. You need to use this sparingly or it can become annoying.

Although this is really a matter of personal taste, both of us have chosen to have our LinkedIn updates duplicated on Twitter, but not vice versa.

Endorsements and recommendations

When you create your profile on LinkedIn you will be asked to list any specific skills that you have. When your connections visit your profile (and sometimes just when they log onto their own account) your connections will see a message asking them to confirm that you have those skills and if they agree that you do, then this counts as an endorsement. You will be sent a message saying that a connection has endorsed you and a list of people endorsing you appears at the end of your LinkedIn profile page. So, all to the good. If you can speak for others and confirm their specific skills from your own experience and knowledge of them then you should do so. You will often find that they reciprocate by endorsing you. Endorsements are quite a useful way of staying in touch with your connections.

Recommendations are rather more powerful. While an endorsement just requires a mouse click, a recommendation is a personal written endorsement from someone for whom you have carried out some work. It's just like a formal written reference. Collecting these is both important and valuable. Why? Recently, we were running a training session for a group of accountants and using a live demonstration of LinkedIn. One of the attendees said that there was one major competitor she had in her home city. Time and again it would be between her and this "foe" as to who won particular pieces of work. We suggested that we look at the LinkedIn profile of the competitor – to our great surprise we found not just a well put together Profile but 84 (yes eighty four) recommendations for him. That was the most that we had ever seen. Our attendee had 2 recommendations.

Imagine the thinking of any potential client faced with two possible professionals who then checked out their LinkedIn profiles – the client is going to be strongly influenced when he or she reads 84 individually created recommendations as opposed to just 2. If fact it meant that the competitor could actively use the recommendations as a way of promoting his services – for example by directing a potential client to the written recommendation of another client for a similar piece of work that had been successfully completed. How powerful is that?

It is not entirely obvious how to either give a recommendation in LinkedIn, nor how to request one. As the layout changes from time the time the easiest way to find out about them is often to go to the help center (American website, American spelling) in LinkedIn and search on the word "recommendation". The help center is found by clicking on the thumbnail of you at the top of the page when you are logged in. At the time of writing you give a recommendation by:

- Go to your Profile (hover your mouse over it) then Edit Profile

- Scroll down to the **Recommendations** box and click the Edit icon.

- Click **Manage Visibility** which you will find under **Your Recommendations** on the right side of the page.

- Click the **Given** tab and scroll down to the **Make a recommendation** section.

- Click "select from your Connections list" and click a name.

- Click the button next to Colleague, Service Provider, Business Partner, or Student and click **Continue**.

- Complete the recommendation form.

- Click **Send**

You can also request recommendations from this area of LinkedIn or just send an email asking for one. Key lesson – if you just completed a great piece of work for someone, ask for a recommendation straight away. When you receive one you can decide whether or not to display it on your profile – it doesn't display there automatically.

Job changes

It goes without saying that you should keep your profile fully up to date and keep polishing it. We have ours diarised to revisit every three months. Something that you will see coming across your news feed is when connections of yours change jobs. That might be a promotion at their existing place of work or a complete move. This is always a great opportunity for you to send congratulations and maybe arrange to meet up with a connection that you haven't seen in a while. Business friendships are just like any other type of friendship, if they are neglected they will wither away.

In addition, LinkedIn will send you a reminder every so often, listing connections of yours that have changed jobs. This is a good chance to run through these and see if you missed any changes that you should now be following up.

Searching on a target

A crucial part of LinkedIn! You can of course find people who might be of value to you just by typing in your interests in the search box and see who comes up. Or you may have come across a target because they were in the news, spoke at a conference that you attended or came to your attention in some other way. You should not try to connect to these people just by sending them an invitation to connect through LinkedIn.

We both receive lots of these invites to connect from "unknowns" and we never say yes to them. LinkedIn is about connecting with people that you already know. But by searching on a target in LinkedIn (a company or a person) then you will likely be given a list of intermediaries. These are people who know the target and are connected to you. In practice, we find that 2nd connections work well (but not 3rd or more). As we saw, a 2nd connection means that the target person is known to someone who is your 1st connection. So that makes it relatively easy to connect. You just ask your 1st connection for an **in**troduction.

Jobs

LinkedIn is very much set up for job searching and in fact there is a lot of activity on the employer side, posting job vacancies and also paying to advertise these jobs so that they appear on the home pages of likely candidates. So it also makes a great place for people who are looking for work or to move to a different company. There is a "Jobs" tab on the front page of LinkedIn and clicking on that takes you to a page of suggested jobs and a search box. You can use that search box to type in a type of work (e.g. "brand strategy") or a sector ("Energy") or a specific company at which you would like to work. All of these will bring up a long list of suggestions. Helpfully, under each job there will be an indication of any connections that you have in the relevant company. If you have some 1st Connections then that's easy. You already know these people so you can make contact with them. It can be just as useful if you find 2nd connections as it means that someone you know can introduce you.

We think it's really important how you approach these connections if they turn up on a job search. In particular we don't think it is good practice to ask them to get you the job or to influence the selection in your favour. Most companies have lots of procedures in place to stop that type of nepotism. However, your connections can be of real help, for example, if they work in the relevant company (or can introduce you to someone who does) because you can ask the relevant person to give you a little time on the phone or over coffee to get a feel for what it is like working there. What are the core values of the company, what it is really good at, who are their key competitors and how do they beat them?

If you can get face time with someone who works at the company that you are interested in, then it gives you a great opportunity to feel the working environment and hopefully meet some of their people. The purpose of your call or visit should be made really clear. You are thinking of applying for a job at that company and you wanted to really understand what it is like to work there, before you apply. That's a safe and reasonable approach. There must not be any undertone of trying to circumvent the recruitment process or to use your connections to try to win the job. People are generally happy to talk about their work and their employer. Approached in this way, as an information gathering exercise, then it can work really well. A great way to end any conversation, is to ask the other person if there is anyone else in the company that you should talk to as well. For example they might be able to put you in contact with someone in the HR team (a great question to them is "what two things are absolute essentials for the candidates for this job"). This helps to see if you have any required qualities or qualifications for the role. Or your connection might be able to put you in contact with someone closer to the relevant department who could fill you in with more detail about the role or the type of person that they are seeking. All wonderful background information that will help you to prepare a great application.

Don't forget to also revisit your profile and make sure that it covers (even emphasises) the qualities and qualifications that you have that make you particularly suitable for the job in question.

Finally, have a look at some of the job seeker premium products offered by LinkedIn. These are available on a monthly basis and can help you to find out about relevant jobs offered via LinkedIn. If you are in the market for a job, or to change jobs, then you might also make an exception to the general rule that you only connect to people that you actually know. One of the general facts of life on LinkedIn is that head hunters and recruiters will ask to connect to people that they do not know. This is so that they can build up their list of potential candidates.

So you might say yes to these people, even if you do not know them. Once they have connected to you, they will be able to access your email address and contact you further. So you might want to change your default email address if you are seeking to change jobs! You can always remove this head-hunter connection (just like you can any connection) at a future date by going to your full list of connections whilst logged in, right clicking a connection and under the word "other" you will find the option to remove them. We also use this if someone that we are connected to starts over using the status update box. It is an easy matter to remove a connection and they are not sent any notification that you have done so.

For those who are looking for their first job, it is good practice to start your Profile by saying "currently looking to work in the energy sector, particularly in Geothermal Energy" to flag up that you are very much open to offers.

Twitter

A vast, and rapidly growing, open conversation that has the potential to connect you not just better within your own circle, but give you access to breaking news, thought leaders and share thoughts and ideas with interesting individuals (future contacts) all across the world. A lot of people worry about "not knowing know what to do" – they think because it's new social media or "for young people" that it's difficult, when in truth, it's just an open and interactive conversation.

Often we hear people say "I don't have time for twitter" or "I don't see the point, I don't care what Joe Bloggs has to say" – yes it takes time to tweet, but actually, it can also save you time by connecting you directly to your preferred news sources and industry thought leaders, who, chances are if they're any good, will have their own Twitter account.

What's first?

There are two key concepts to keep in mind when looking at the networking benefits of Twitter. The first is "personal brand" and the second is "size". Twitter is a great way of building your brand (potentially across the world!), increasing your recognition and building your brand values. But the effect is going to pass unnoticed unless you build up your followers so that you have a real impact in your chosen area.

So your first step is to follow and to acquire followers. To follow is easy. Find people to follow by using search terms that are relevant to you. On the home page of Twitter (or while using the app) use the search field to find specific people or companies that you would like to follow. Or type in words relevant to your interests to find others who share those interests and then follow them as well. At first, it is advisable to follow as many people and companies as you can find because you can easily refine your choices later by unfollowing any that turn out to be irrelevant.

With the benefit of following numerous relevant people, you can get a feel for issues relevant to your chosen area and join in the conversation. Just like being involved in Groups on LinkedIn this is a great way of raising your own profile as well.

How to join in

There are a number of ways to take part in conversations and be seen as part of the group. First, you can yourself make comments on issues affecting your interests by Tweeting and adding hash tags that highlight your interests:

"Great article - unspoilt Caribbean Isle using #geothermal energy to preserve the #environment http://bit.ly/1a1IC0p"

This Tweet references two relevant hash tags so that others with your interests will be able to find this, and uses the web site www.bit.ly to shorten the web address of the relevant web page.

Next, you can retweet (RT) any incoming Tweets that you receive (based on the people or companies that you are following). To do this you click on the button on Twitter that is made up of two arrows following each other around a square - this means that this Tweet will now appear in your own Twitter feed so that anyone who follows you will now see it. When accessing Twitter through different ways, such as the app rather than web browser, you have the further option when retweeting to 'quote tweet' where you can add your own comment. You can obviously directly respond the person / company that made the original Tweet (and anyone who retweeted it) by clicking the single arrow link under the Tweet, often it can be an easy way to have a light interaction with someone and build up familiarity. When tweeting, do remember that whatever you say in tweets, retweets or replies are not private and will be displayed to anyone publicly on your own Twitter profile page (unless you have a private account, which stops anyone not pre-approved from seeing your profile, but also cuts down on your ability to openly interact). When you both follow each other, there is also the option to DM (Direct Message) people, 140 character messages sent privately and only viewable by the two of you (useful for swapping further contact information). Alternatively, you can just mark a tweet as a "Favourite" by clicking on the star icon underneath it.

As you can see, creating your own tweets and responding to those that you follow starts to create traffic and presence. Quite often, when you follow someone that has a common interest with you, they will follow you back. If your own tweets are interesting (and particularly if you are really adding value, giving out valuable content and references) then your followers will retweet your tweets which gives them a much larger audience and should lead to more people deciding to follow you.

This leads to your building up your own number of followers and that starts to become really valuable. Bear in mind that it is not just the absolute numbers here that are important. Done well, your followers will have shared interests with you. This makes them more likely to be interested in you and your comments and more inclined to offer help.

The value of followers

Followers are a measure of your online brand – how big a profile you have online. Someone who has built up several thousand followers through Twitter has created a valuable resource and your "digital footprint" is an issue of increasing importance to recruiters and clients. If you are an expert in an area of interest, or if you aspire to be, then having built up a following is a real sign of your commitment and perseverance. You do need to devote time to Twitter if you are going to maintain a serious online brand. Whilst it is unlikely to be a huge drain on your time, you need to be disciplined in actually Tweeting regularly if you are to maintain interest.

One great way to help build your number of followers is to look out for trending stories on Twitter and ride on the back of them. You can see "Trending" on Twitter.com or inside the app – look out for subjects that have some link to your own topics of interest and Tweet using both hashtags in your Tweet. All those people who are tracking the trending stories will also be served up with your Tweet. Don't stretch the link too far or you will just annoy, but do look for opportunities to link your own interests with trending topics.

How else can you use Twitter?

Building a following gives you other opportunities. If you have a blog or a website, then you can use Tweets to drive traffic to these. It can also be a great way to meet people in real life by tweeting your attendance at industry events, seminars and the like – many conferences and summit meetings often have a live 'tweet feed' so you can give real-time feedback and share your thoughts. Your followers can also be the most amazing source of help and advice. Having built up followers from your key interests, they are in the best position to help you by giving advice or making introductions.

So our overview – Twitter cannot compete with LinkedIn in terms of business efficacy, but it can form a really useful part of your online strategy and be an important part of who you are and how well you are known online.

TEN

WHY HELPING OTHERS WORKS

Do you remember your early birthday parties when you were in school? There was a very simple rule – if Anton invites me to his birthday party then I must invite him to mine. If Jennifer buys me a present, then I should buy her one in return. These simple rules are in fact deeply ingrained at a societal level. As you got older friends might invite you to a dinner party at their place and you know that this means holding a dinner party so that you can invite them back.

The rule of reciprocity

You may not have realised this at the time, but what you were seeing at work here was the principle of reciprocity. You should give back to others the behaviour that they first give to you. It is a powerful, intuitive force. It is hard to resist, although of course you will come across the occasional person who has mastered the art of taking without giving in return. Don't let that put you off. These people are quite easily spotted and avoided. For everyone else, reciprocity is a great way of receiving help that you didn't expect.

There has been much academic research around the principle of reciprocity. Perhaps the best known was conducted by Professor Robert Cialdini of Arizona State University, who is renowned for his book "Influence" which studied this and the other ways that one human being can use to try to persuade another human to follow a particular course of action. In a series of experiments, Cialdini was able to show that people who gave first fared much better than those who didn't. The principle can be refined into a series of rules:

- You must give first. Otherwise you are not creating an obligation, you are returning a favour.

- You must give freely, not with the intention of creating a debt of obligation. People can spot the difference, particularly where a gift is out of proportion. Such a gift is more likely to be refused, rather than to work as reciprocity.

- The help you give, or gift you offer, must be tailored to the person receiving it. So, it's great to say "I remembered you mentioning that you were going on holiday to Miami, so I'm passing on the Guide Book I used when I visited there last year". But it's not good to say "I'm going to watch my favourite football team so I bought an extra ticket for you." That would make the gift *about you and your interests, not about the person receiving it.* In fact tailored gifts are doubly valuable because they show that you were listening to what the other person was saying and that you are *interested in them* (remember that?)

Reciprocity is also a great approach for any professional person because it doesn't involve any selling, marketing or asking for favours. Professional people are rarely excited by selling skills as they feel that it cuts across the professional relationship. Are you a trusted adviser or are you just trying to sell something to clients. There is often a natural aversion to selling, even if it is selling yourself. But there is an equally strong desire *to help* people. So using reciprocity is a way of reframing the desire of a professional person to grow existing clients and to win new clients. Reciprocity says "help others and reciprocity will lead to you getting more business". But don't just help these people by doing your usual day job, after all that's what you are paid for. Rather, network into people who have shared interests and look for ways to help them. It is, genuinely, as simple as that. What could possibly go wrong? Just as importantly, particularly for introverts, knowing that your motivation is solely to offer help to the people that you meet, removes a lot of the pressure of networking. After all, the worst thing that can happen to someone that you meet is that you have them talk about themselves and, if you can find a way to help them, then you will. No pressure to achieve anything "salesy" from networking. You can rely on the principle of reciprocity to reward you for your giving behaviour.

Serendipity

This word, meaning unexpected good fortune, may be the real secret behind networking and reciprocity. We saw how Professor Robert Cialdini showed that giving must be without any expectation of return if it is to bring the real benefits of reciprocation. Imagine that you need regulatory approval to build a new home and a friend of yours is appointed regulator. What would it feel like if you turned up at a meeting with a case of vintage champagne? It would look like a bribe, like an attempt to curry favour and influence a future decision. Because that's exactly what it is. It's a gift given in expectation of a valuable return.

You must give freely and ideally to people whom you didn't realise could help you. Here's how we think it works:

- When you give freely, you range widely. By not being calculating and trying to work out which people are going to be most valuable to your future life, you end up being helpful to a disparate group of people, but your focus will concentrate a lot of your attention upon people who share your interests.

- The people that you help will all have a great impression of you. They mentioned something to you and you found a way of being helpful.

- This creates karma, goodwill and an obligation of reciprocity in the receivers.

- We all like to help other people. Imagine you spent last weekend putting up shelves at home for the first time. On your third visit to the DIY store for necessary equipment you come across a laser level which projects an exactly straight line onto your wall enabling you to vastly improve your success rate. Then, a week later one of your friends tells you they have to spend *their* weekend putting up shelves. Aren't you going to proffer your "expert" advice and lend your friend the laser level?

- For both of us, the most valuable gifts that we have to give to other people are introductions to the friends that we meet through our networking activities. Most of the time, the help that we give to people that we meet is to introduce them to someone we already know. What an amazing gift to be able to give to someone a real, live, human being. So we might say, "If you are interested in Geothermal Energy, you must meet Joost", or, "If you are having issues pricing professional services then talk to Kevin", or, "Starting to teach students online – talk to Michele"; or, "You are addicted to avocados? I'm going to introduce you to Alexis". We do this *all the time*.

- People love being connected to others with the same interests, people who share their passions or just people that they can help. A typical introduction like this means that there are *two people* who feel a sense of obligation, a sense of reciprocity towards us.

- This creates a growing band of humans who both like us and who would like to be able to help us in return. That's where serendipity steps in. You simply cannot predict which of these people will have the opportunity to repay your kindness by doing you a big favour. What you can be sure of, is that the more often that you do this, the bigger the pool of people who are really well inclined towards you and are looking for an opportunity to help you back. You simply put yourself in the firing line for good luck and it will find you.

Here's another way of looking at it. Imagine that you are born into a world where every other person wants to help *you*. That's pretty amazing isn't it? Imagine how differently your life will unfold with the whole world of humans all working to help you achieve your goals and desires. This is what you create by being a "giver" when you meet other people. Not only is it pleasant for other people to meet you, but these people also feel an obligation of reciprocity to help you in return. You create a universe of helpers. Add to that a focus, an area of interest, and you transform the chances of achieving your goals. Don't think of this as "you scratch my back and I will scratch yours". That mentality is measured and cautious and will be directed only to those whom you believe can help you and they will surely perceive your motivations.

The concept of "giving first, without the need for return" is somewhat philosophical. It is pretty much a life choice. Those who choose this path will tell you that it brings rewards many times its cost. Not just in terms of career objectives but in building a supportive community of friends. It is worth also considering the opposite approach. If you put your own needs first and look at others for what you can take from them. In which case you may find that they treat you in the same way.

In Keith Ferrazzi's words as he paraphrases the one and only Dale Carnegie: "You can be more successful in two months by becoming really interested in other people's success, than you can in two years trying to get more people interested in your own success."

So tell me, now, what can I do for you?

But there is another method!

A few years ago there was an amazing discussion thread that went viral and led to the argument that there are actually two types of people in the world. It occurred when Andrea Donderi replied to an Ask MetaFilter question about etiquette which was this, "A friend of your husband / wife / live in partner, is coming to town on a business trip for two weeks and asks if he can sleep in your spare room while he is in town. How do you reply assuming that you think this is a bit cheeky and you really want to say no?" Andrea said that basically there are two types of people in the world.

"This is a classic case of Ask Culture meets Guess Culture. In some families, you grow up with the expectation that it's OK to ask for anything at all, but you gotta realize you might get no for an answer. This is Ask Culture.

In Guess Culture, you avoid putting a request into words unless you're pretty sure the answer will be yes. Guess Culture depends on a tight net of shared expectations. A key skill is putting out delicate feelers. If you do this with enough subtlety, you won't even have to make the request directly; you'll get an offer. Even then, the offer may be genuine or pro forma; it takes yet more skill and delicacy to discern whether you should accept."

The trouble occurs when an "asker" meets a "guesser". The asker feels free to ask for anything they want or need, the guesser feels put upon and embarrassed at having to come up with more and more inventive ways to say no. In fact, the views expressed in the discussion thread were that the answer to this problem is for the person being asked for this (big) favour to say "no, that won't work for me" or "no, I can't do that" without giving any explanation, because the asker was kind of expecting that you would say no anyway.

There can be cultural differences as well. "Polite" countries, particularly those in Asia, may be much more inclined towards a "guessing approach" and will find askers to be rude and presumptuous. Askers can be frustrated at guessers as they are not at all clear about what they want. So how should you behave? The problem is that both approaches bring results and people really do seem to be hard wired into one behaviour or another (although to varying degrees of strength). Here's our advice:

If you are an asker:

If you are dealing with people in one off situations then ask away. Askers receive upgrades on flights, better hotel rooms and extras in stores just for asking. No doubt about it. Of course you will also garner lots of refusals, but that doesn't bother you, because you were expecting that weren't you?

But, if you are with friends and business contacts then beware of "Charity Fatigue" a well-recognised syndrome where people can just tire of always giving. If you don't make sure that you give as often as you take, then you can build a reputation as a taker which will cause people to avoid you and your calls. So be careful what you ask for. Is it for some advice (which is flattering to the other person) or is it for something pretty substantial.

Be sensitive to cultural differences. Asking may be acceptable behaviour in northern European Countries and North America, but won't be welcomed in Southern Europe or Asia – give first!

Here's a useful exercise for you. Think about your Connections on LinkedIn and try giving first. Make sure you have some "gives" every week.

If you are a guesser:

You are missing out on some great perks. Better rooms in hotels, the corner table in restaurants and a free shirt to go with the suit that you just bought. So this is a great place to start, with people you aren't going to meet again. You can start by asking for something extra like an upgraded hotel room at check in or ringing around several hotels to find the best rate they have "Surely that's not the best that you can give me, if I book directly with you".

Mary Beaulieu, Assistant Dean at the Harvard Kennedy School of Government, gives the following great advice – "why not ask for something small each day?"

Give yourself permission to ask and make sure that it's not something important. Just ask for something each day and you will start to learn how to ask and not to feel bad with the occasional "no". From these small successes you will gain confidence and learn that you don't always have to guess".

Where can this take you?

The real joy of networking and reciprocity is that there is absolutely no limit to where it can take you. When Kevin decided that he wanted to work at Universities after his career inside a law firm, he told his good friend Reena Sengupta of RSG Consulting who researches the Financial Times Innovation Awards. She said – "Oh, if you are interested in Universities then you should meet my friend Moray McLaren. He's an Associate Professor at IE Law School in Madrid and developed the Lawyers Management Program for them." Kevin volunteered to teach some sessions on that Program and Moray introduced Kevin to Professor Michele DeStefano at Miami University who had created the amazing LawWithoutWalls Program. Kevin volunteered to teach networking on that program, travelling to St Gallen in Switzerland and Miami to take part and support LawWithoutWalls. Months later Kevin was in Boston at the same time as Michele, who invited Kevin to lunch with Professor Ashish Nanda at Harvard Law School. Over lunch Ashish asked Kevin about his areas of interest which led to Ashish mentoring Kevin through the creation of the Harvard Law School Case Study on pricing and to Kevin joining their Faculty of Executive Education as a Visiting Professor and teaching at Harvard.

When Kevin was asked by the London School of Economics to teach Networking and Personal Brand he asked his friends for help and they suggested that Alexis, as a Brand Strategist, could help to design the training. Alexis volunteered to help and gave his time for free to teach at the LSE. Some months later, Alexis was working in New York when Kevin was in Boston and planning to have dinner with Michele who was there visiting Harvard. So they all join in a meal and Michele asked Alexis to join the Faculty at LawWithoutWalls and teach personal brand. Which led to Alexis teaching in St Gallen University in Switzerland (who host the kick off sessions) and to present in a room with 100+ of the most influential people in the world and students from every Continent.

This is one really important point to note about this story. *No one had a job to give!* There were no jobs for which Kevin or Alexis could have applied! Meeting people and helping them leads to opportunities that you could not have known existed. But you must have a passion, you must have interests in common and you must be prepared to give freely.

Then you can sit back and enjoy the ride...

APPENDICES

Practical tech advice for the online world.

APPENDIX I

OPENING A NEW ACCOUNT ON LINKEDIN

NOTE: LinkedIn regularly updates the content of its site and the layout of its pages. The instructions in this Appendix are accurate at the time of writing. If you have any difficulties then you can go to the Help Center on LinkedIn and type in questions directly.

Xing.com is a similar networking site that is also strong in some countries – if this applies to you then it may be appropriate to join that or to join both Xing and LinkedIn.

Starting on LinkedIn

Go to www.LinkedIn.com and you will see an option to "Join LinkedIn Today" where you just need to fill in your name, your email address and to choose a password that you will use with LinkedIn. (Once you have an account you log in using the email address and password you just gave). Make sure that you choose a specific password for LinkedIn – not the same one that you use for the email address that you are using.

After you have done that you will be taken to the first page of "Building your Profile" where it asks for your Country and Post Code, and also whether you are currently employed, a job seeker or a student. If you are employed you need to add your current position and the name of your employer – interestingly as you start to type that, LinkedIn suggest company names based upon the data and company pages it is already holding. If you are employed you add details of the industry sector that you are in and then click "Create Profile".

The next step can use the email address you gave to search your email contacts to suggest people that you might want to connect with (or you can just skip this step). IMPORTANT NOTE – we strongly recommend that you DO NOT allow LinkedIn to search through your email addresses to look for connections. The reason for this is that there are complaints online from people who allowed this, then because they did not carefully examine the options on every subsequent page, ended up with LinkedIn emailing everyone they had ever had any contact with and asking them to connect. You can open up your email contacts to LinkedIn and still avoid any unwelcome invites going out if you are careful, but our advice is that this in not currently worth the risk and should be avoided. If you decide to skip this step (as we recommend) then on the next page you are given another chance to access the contacts of this email address (!) but you can avoid this by clicking "Send a confirmation email instead".

If you choose the confirmation email route (so that LinkedIn doesn't access your contacts) you then need to pick up that email from your email account, click to confirm that it's your email address and then you will be taken to a normal LinkedIn sign in screen where you just enter your email address and password that you chose for LinkedIn and you will be taken to the screen that says "Let's start customizing your experience with us". Once again you have the opportunity to let LinkedIn access your email contacts to start building connections (!!) which you accept by clicking the "Continue" button that appears under your email address. Or you can skip this (again) *which is what we recommend* by clicking on the words "Next step" that appear bottom right on the page. Let's do that.

The next page list some possible Groups for you to join based upon the information that you gave so far. If you like any of the suggested Groups then you can join by clicking on them, otherwise it is very easy to join Groups later on. Let's assume we choose to skip the suggested Groups in which case we will click on "Next step" when you will be taken to some suggested people that you might like to follow. This is not like following on other social networks in the sense that LinkedIn choose which people can be followed (it's quite a select few) and these are high profile Businessmen and Businesswomen and Thought Leaders.

Click on any that you want to follow and then "Next step" takes you to a page where there are some suggestions of Companies that you might want to follow. Companies are able to set up their own pages on LinkedIn and very many have. You can follow any company. Choose any that you want (or none) from the suggestions made by LinkedIn and then choose "Next step". You will have the opportunity then to have a confirmation email sent to the email address that you chose, and when you click on the link on that you will have yet another opportunity to access your email contacts to look for connections (!!!) and if you skip that (AS WE RECOMMEND) you are then given a page of "People you may know" as a final stage. You might be surprised at how good some of these suggestions are! Pick any that you know and want to connect with, and you are done.

Your standard welcome page

Once you have completed the steps above, then you are taken to the standard front page that is now going to welcome you whenever you log into LinkedIn. At the top is yet another opportunity to allow LinkedIn to access your email contacts so that it can suggest people that you can connect to on LinkedIn (!!!). You just have to become used to that.

You will also see the typical areas of information that appear and are discussed in detail in Chapter 9 of this book – The News Feed (where you see updates and information from your Connections and Groups plus random adverts and updates from thought leaders etc.)

Top right on the page you will see suggestions of "People you may know" – and clicking on those words will bring up page after page of suggestions. Often worth a look and the more Connections that you make, the more accurate the suggestions will be.

Underneath this will be information on people who have looked at your Profile on LinkedIn (will be blank if you only just joined) and suggestion of jobs that may interest you and Companies that you might like to follow, and so on.

Top and centre on the page you will find a blank box which you can fill in with Updates that you want to share with your Connections – to which you can add a picture, video, slide set or link. Details on using that are in Chapter 9.

For now it is important that we start thinking about Your Profile and editing that. So click on the word "Profile" at the top of the page and choose "Edit Profile"

Creating your background and Profile

You are now taken to a key page that starts enabling you to give some really important information about you. At the top of the page it starts by asking you questions about your current job if you are employed. On the page you will find links to the many areas that need completing to give details about your studies, your areas of interest and so on. The more of these that you are able to complete the better – both so that people can see what your main areas of interest and focus are and also so they can see what you have in common with them (crucial for creating empathy with them).

Let's look at how to fill in many of these blanks and remember that it is very easy on LinkedIn to look at other peoples Profiles (just search on their names in the search box that appears at the top of every page on LinkedIn) and then you can find ideas from others. Do bear in mind though that every time you look at someone's Profile you leave a "track' so they will be able to see that you were looking at them the next time that they log in. You can switch off "tracks" in the Privacy Settings – we look at how to do that below.

Here is a list of areas that you can complete:

1. Add a photo. Click the picture icon to choose a self-picture and upload it. You should be smiling, but in work clothes / mode. Just have a look at a few other people's Profile pictures if you are not sure.

2. Summary. Really important because it is often the first thing that people see if they search on you (whether from inside LinkedIn or using a search engine like Google or Bing). This is where you start by describing your areas of focus / passion. You can be pretty emotional about this if it feels right for you – there are some great Profiles that start "From an early age I knew that I wanted a career in ……". Make sure that you use "I" and don't write it in the third person using "He" or "She"

3. Experience. A chance to talk about activities and work that you have carried out. Again have a look at people that you know for ideas but don't worry too much about this if it is early on in your career – what is more important at that stage is what your key interests are – as set out in the Summary.

4. Education. Be realistic here. University graduate and post graduate courses are appropriate as is other formal training. Your school record is unlikely to be of relevance.

5. Skills – you can claim up to 50 "Skills" – as you start typing them in then LinkedIn will suggest options. The relevance of skills is twofold. First, if you have a specific job related skill (which might be proficiency in Excel or PowerPoint) or actual experience gained through your work then you

should be stating that. It is much used by head-hunters and recruitment agencies when searching for candidates. Secondly, your Connections have an opportunity to "Endorse" you for a skill – which is to say that, from their knowledge of you, they agree that you have that skill or those skills. You can claim up to 50 – we think it's better to focus upon the ones that are important to you and to your future career rather than going overboard on numbers of skills.

6.   Languages – yes complete this and give details if you have some proficiency (you don't need to be fluent).

When you look around this page you will see lots of other options – for example, "Courses attended", "Honors and Awards", "Volunteering and Causes". Just complete as many as you can. The more complete a Profile looks, the more impressive it is. Certainly, a Profile with a lot of blank gaps looks a bit half hearted.

Privacy and Account Settings

A much neglected area is whether you accept all the default Privacy and Account Settings or whether to change some. This is very much a matter of personal choice, here are thoughts on some of the most important ones. You reach the settings page by hovering your mouse over the picture of you that appears top right on your home page (if you haven't uploaded a photo yet then it shows a silhouette) and choosing Privacy + Settings – Review, from the menu that appears. You will be asked to input your password again for security and will then be presented with a page full of options. It is worth looking at each of these in turn. There are a lot of options and some of them have quite substantial effects.

The first batch of options appears next to the heading "Your Profile" and current option are:

Turn on/off your activity broadcasts

By default, when you change anything on your Profile, make a recommendation (i.e. you write a written recommendation about someone who did some great work for you – see Chapter 9) or follow a company then in the Activity Feed (that by default is sent to all of your Connections) a message saying what you did is displayed. So it might say that you "Updated your Profile", "Added a skill" or "changed your Profile picture". So here's a thought. At the early stage when you have lots of work to do on building up the details of your Profile you might want this *switched off* as otherwise, every time you make a change, all of your Connections will be told that. So our advice is that for the first few weeks, while you create and complete your Profile you switch this off (just click on it, un-tick the box and click save) and that you switch it back on once you have finished this work.

Select who can see your activity broadcast

The default for this is "Your Connections". This means that they are the ones who see what you write in the blank box that appears on your home page. That is sensible. If you are just trying something out then you could change this to "Only you", but this is probably best left unchanged. There are two other options. "Everyone" which seems surprising. Let's assume you would never use that. There is also an option of "Your network" – LinkedIn defines your network as being your Connections (meaning people that you are directly connected to – also called 1st Connections) plus 2nd degree Connections (people who are connected to your 1st Connections) plus 3rd Connections (people who are connected to your second connections) plus the people who are in any Groups that you have joined. That's a lot of people.

It's probably best to keep this at the default setting of "Your Connections". Even if the activity broadcast is turned off, your Connections will still be notified if you change your profile picture.

Select what others see when you've viewed their Profile

This is what we refer to by "leaving tracks" – whenever you look at someone's Profile in LinkedIn while you are logged in to your account you leave a track and they will receive a message on their Home Page saying that you viewed their Profile. Some people leave this at the default setting on the basis that they are quite happy that other people see that they were interested in them – it can lead to that person offering to connect.

You can switch this off in two ways – click on it and you are offered the option to be anonymous but to give some details of your occupation, company or location – in that case it might say as a track "Someone at Coca Cola" viewed your Profile, or "A Director at University of Miami" viewed your Profile. Quite often this "half-way house" of anonymity isn't very anonymous. The final option is to be fully anonymous, in which case the notification given to the person whose Profile was viewed will say "LinkedIn Member" viewed your Profile.

If you choose either of these two methods of hiding your identity then (as a classic account free member) you will also lose the ability to see who viewed your Profile. If you upgrade to a paid account then you gain the ability to switch off your tracks, whilst still being able to see who has viewed your Profile.

Select who can see your Connections

By default, once you connect to someone, they will be able to look at all of the other Connections that you have and likewise you can see all of their Connections. You can change this to "Only you" which makes your Connections private. Up to you. Some people say that they are proud of their Connections and are happy for anyone to whom they connect to also look at them – they might even find someone to whom they would like to be introduced.

Others feel that this is too open and that their Connections are a private matter. Easy to switch one way or the other anyway.

Change your profile photo and visibility

You can use this setting to upload a photo or to change it. At the same time it can also be used to choose who can see your photo with the choices being "Your Connections", "Your network" or "Anyone". Probably best to leave this as "Your Connections" as the others are really big numbers of people.

Show/hide "Viewers of this profile also viewed" box

Self-explanatory really. Decide if you want that information displayed to you or not.

Manage your Twitter settings

Useful option this. You can add your Twitter account to LinkedIn so that anything that you tweet also appears on your LinkedIn activity broadcast and / or any update that you share using the box on your home page of LinkedIn (or the first 140 characters of it) will also be added to your Twitter feed.

A good way of achieving two hits in one. Something to watch out for is that if you are using the box on your home page to share an update and to include a link to a web page then you may need to use a web address shortening service (like bitly.com or goo.gl) so that the address will still fit within the 140 character limit.

Other settings

The settings referred to above are important to address and think about. Once you are in the "Privacy and Settings" area you will find a lot more. Just have a quick look and you can decide if there are some that are particularly relevant to you.

LINKEDIN SIGNATURE BLOCK

Outlook

Step 1. You need a "public address"

First you need to access your account settings. At the time of writing (LinkedIn do have a bit of a record of moving this around so you may need to use "Help" in LinkedIn to find this) you just hover your mouse over your picture at top right after you have logged into LinkedIn and a menu appears called "Privacy and Settings". Remember this because it is used for several purposes. For now you just click on this and you need to log in again (for security, just in case you left yourself logged in on someone else's computer) and you are then taken to the main Privacy and Settings Page. You are looking for "Edit your public Profile" which is currently on the right hand side about half way down the page. When you follow this link you will find on the far right at the bottom of the page the option to "Customize your public Profile URL". In other words, when you first opened a LinkedIn account it generated a URL for you which is just a specific web address that you could cut and paste and use as a direct link to your public Profile. You have the opportunity to customise this (subject to availability) – for example to simplify it (subject to availability) to include your surname - http://uk.linkedin.com/in/[yoursurname]

Step 2. A URL and a Badge

Once you have this URL then you can add it to your email signature (as explained below) and it will appear as a link that anyone receiving an email from you can click to be taken to your public Profile. LinkedIn has a neater way of arranging this by allowing you to cut and paste its logo as a "badge" – then anyone clicking on the badge which has on it the words "view my Profile on LinkedIn" is taken directly to your public Profile. First, make a note of the URL of your public Profile (customised by you if you wish) and then click on the link (bottom right of the page) which says "Create a Profile badge". That takes you to a page of badges so that you can choose the exact one that you prefer. Next to each badge is the corresponding HTML code. This may not be as useful as it looks (as we wanted to add a signature, not add a link on a web page) so we just right clicked the badge that we wanted and chose "Copy" so that we held a copy of it before the next stage.

Step 3. Create an email signature in Outlook

In Outlook you create or amend email signatures by opening a new email message and then choosing "Insert" and choosing Signatures. This allows you to create a signature (if you don't already have one) or amend an existing one by adding your LinkedIn information. So, for example, if you had an existing Signature you would choose it (Standard) then you would use drop down boxes that choose to use it both when creating a new email and replying to an email. You then type in the details that you want – name, contact telephone numbers and so on, and then at the bottom of that you paste the LinkedIn badge that you just chose and copied to your clipboard.

Step 4. The hyperlink in Outlook

The final stage is then to click on this badge to make sure it is highlighted as active and then click on the hyperlink button that is at the top of this box (it's a picture of a globe). That opens another box (Insert Hyperlink) with a blank line that allows you to type in the URL – so you just type in the URL of your public Profile (or cut and paste it from the LinkedIn settings) into the line saying "Address" Click OK and you are done. You are now displaying a LinkedIn badge at the foot of your email signature and the badge has an embedded hyperlink so anyone clicking on it is taken directly to your public Profile. It took a bit of doing but the effect is well worth it.

Mac Mail

You can follow a similar route in Mac OS to add the URL of your public profile as part of your email signature (although according to the LinkedIn Help Center you cannot add a logo as Mac Mail does not support this). Open an email, type in your signature, add your URL (or words like "see my LinkedIn Profile") highlight the URL / the words that you typed, right click on them and follow Link / Add Link, enter your URL in the pop up box and click OK.

APPENDIX III

OPENING A NEW ACCOUNT ON TWITTER

This is easy. Go to www.twitter.com. Enter your full name, and an email address and the password that you want to use for your Twitter Account. On the next page you will be asked to choose a (unique) username – your Twitter Handle. After accepting this you are taken to a quick tutorial of using Twitter and then asked to start "Following" people (Twitter will make suggestions from famous people and people you might know) and then organisations like News Feeds and so on, so that you start your account following a good selection of sources. You are asked to follow 5 of each but you can Skip these steps – it's quite well hidden but there is an option to skip through this.

Next you are asked to search for contacts in your email accounts by logging into them and allowing Twitter to suggest people to follow from your contacts. Up to you whether or not you want to do that. You can skip this by clicking on the "Skip" link that appears (faintly) on the left of the page.

Next you are asked to upload a picture of yourself. Most people so this – make sure it's business appropriate, and you are smiling!

After that you are in. Now confirm your email account by clicking the link you are sent and log in again. This is your chance to edit your profile to say something about you. Look around at others, but the principle is to keep it short. This is an important opportunity for you to flag up your passions / key areas of interest and maybe even your personal brand!

Search on keywords relevant to you and follow people that look like they will be of interest. When you are following someone you are able to message them directly using the "@" symbol in front of their username – although bear in mind these messages are not private and also appear in your Twitter feed.

Tweets are limited to 140 characters but you can add a photo, and can use part of your allocation of 140 to refer to a web site. Because web addresses are often quite long, you can use a service that shortens web addresses like www.bit.ly or www.goo.gl

Just like LinkedIn, try to make sure that your Tweets add value to people reading them. If you have personal Tweets that are intended for your friends and family rather than the business world then our advice is to have two accounts – one personal and one for business, so that you keep your tweets separate.

You can "link" your LinkedIn posts so that they are repeated on your Twitter account (remembering that Twitter will only see the first 140 characters). To do this you need to go into account settings in LinkedIn and add your Twitter account. Then, when you type a status update in LinkedIn you will find the option to display the update in your Twitter feed as well will be available to you.

ABOUT THE AUTHORS

Alexis Caught joined a leading strategy consultancy after completing his degree in Communications and Media Law at Westminster University, working with a specific focus on Insight, Innovation and Strategy within the Nutrition, Health and Wellness Sector.

After several years at Head Office, he relocated to The Netherlands to set up and lead the Insight offer as part of the Strategy team in the Amsterdam Office. There, he worked with a number of consumer, pharma and corporate "A Brands" conducting research and running projects across Europe, South America, China and Russia.

Since returning to London to continue work in innovation and strategy, Alexis is currently Associate Partner at consultancy StrategyFour, delivering training and best practice programmes for FTSE100's and top tier professional services firms. With his background in consumer insight he brings many years of experience to focus on the neuro-economics of the purchasing decision.

He has a particular interest in teaching on student and executive education programmes with his experience including Harvard Law School, London School of Economics, St Gallen University and the LawWithoutWalls program from the University of Miami.

When not in the office Alexis can be found outdoors climbing up stuff, jumping off things and generally getting wet and muddy or working to raise funds and awareness in his role as ambassador for a youth homelessness charity.

@AlexisCaught

Contact: NaturalNetworking@StrategyFour.com for details of training, events and mentoring.

 **Kevin Doolan** is a partner in the Møller Professional Service Firms Group at Churchill College, Cambridge having previously been a partner in Global Law firm Eversheds. As Head of Client Relations, Kevin had particular responsibility for relationships with some of the firm's largest clients. Kevin is the winner of a Financial Times Innovation Award for Client Service and of the Law Society's Excellence Award for Innovation.

His work with Tyco under which Eversheds was appointed sole advisor in more than 30 countries under an innovative fee deal is a Harvard Case Study.

In 2013 Kevin created the Harvard Law School Case Study on the Pricing of Professional Services and is a Visiting Professor teaching business development for professionals and pricing on the Harvard Law School Executive Education Program. He also teaches networking and business development at IE Law School in Madrid, at The London School of Economics, on the leadership programme at The Judge Business School Cambridge and is on Faculty at the University of Miami on the LawWithoutWalls Program.

When not out working with his clients, Kevin can be found helping others (of course!)

@DoolanKevin

Contact: NaturalNetworking@StrategyFour.com for details of training, events and mentoring.

CPSIA information can be obtained at www.ICGtesting.com
Printed in the USA
LVOW07s2035180315

431113LV00007B/58/P